Musique
Librairie
Vidéo
Multimédia

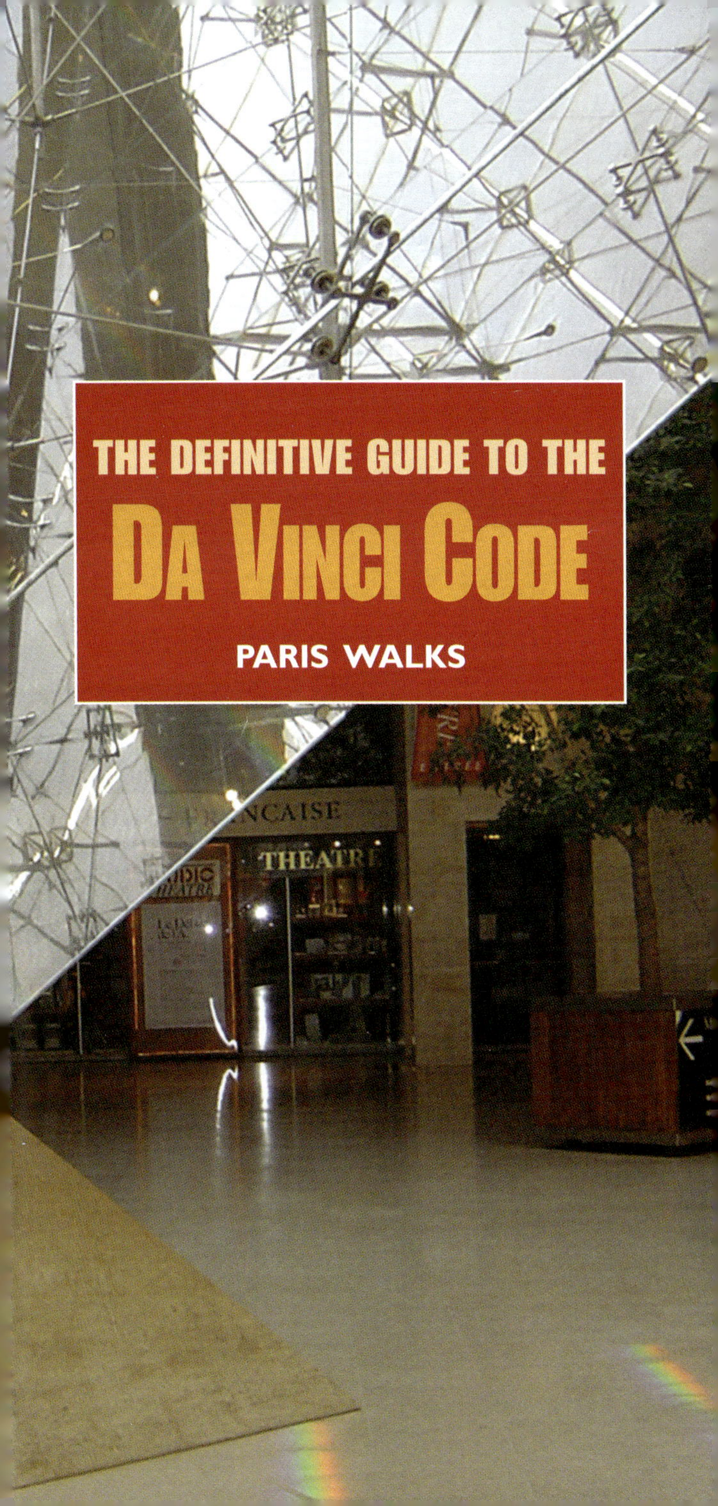

THE DEFINITIVE GUIDE TO THE

DA VINCI CODE

PARIS WALKS

PETER CAINE

THE DEFINITIVE GUIDE TO THE DA VINCI CODE

PARIS WALKS

BARTILLAT
21, rue Servandoni, 75006 Paris

Acknowledgements

No book is written without the help of more people than it is possible to mention.

Special thanks go to Constance de Bartillat and Charles Ficat for the initial idea, and their energy, encouragement, and enthusiasm. Mike at Village Voice for the "Priory" inside story. Marcio for keeping the computers going. The team of guides for keeping Paris Walks going while I was busy researching. Oriel, my wife, for research, proofreading, corrections and putting up with it all. Alain and Valerie for turning it all into French. Thanks also to my family and friends for their encouragement and enthusiasm, and finally to all our clients for whom this guide is written.

Paris Walks

A European Tour Company founded in 1994 – is a real organization. In 1995 Paris' Bibliothèque nationale discovered brochures identifying numerous members of its staff including Peter and Oriel Caine, Brad, Dominique, Edouard, Iris, James, Janice, Jenny, Jonathan, Malcolm, Mary Ellen, Rosemary and Todd.

Paris Walks National Headquarters, costing considerably less than 47 million dollars' is located at 12 passage Meunier in St Denis, 93200, France.

Layout: DVAG, Daniel Verlhac

Illustrations:
All photos © Peter Caine,
except Moulin de la Galette by Matt Spencer,
Château de Villette by permision, and Cryptex by Justin Nevins.
Other documents and objects from the author's collection.

"One of the most common questions I'm asked by readers is where can they go to see all of the art, architecture, locations and symbols described in the book?"

DAN BROWN

"The answer, I hope can be found in this book."

PETER CAINE

Contents

Foreword

This book is for anyone who loves Paris, but especially for those who love to walk its streets with a spirit of discovery. The theme that ties it together is the story told in Dan Brown's best selling thriller *The Da Vinci Code*. In the book, mystifying codes, secret societies, religious sects, religious controversy and mysterious monuments are all clues that lead a trail across Paris and beyond. An irresistible quest just waiting to be followed. Whether you have read the book or not, if you are a keen explorer of the city and its many mysteries, this book is for you. This is how it came about!

My wife and I set up Paris Walks over ten years ago. As art historians our purpose was to bring to life some 2000 years of Paris' history, art and architecture. Literally thousands of people have come on our guided visits to discover the wonders of Paris, its museums, monuments and ancient historic quarters. Some time ago, like so many others, we began to hear frequent references to a new book, some sort of thriller, set in Paris. In the story, the curator of the Louvre was murdered, whilst the pro tagonists departed on a treasure hunt following clues hidden in Da Vinci's paintings. Not the kind of book we usually read! As the months went by I was accosted each time I accompanied a group into St Sulpice Church, and each time I was asked the same questions: "Is there a Rose Line here in the church?" and "Where is the Gnomon?" Eventually my curiosity was aroused enough to acquire the book. I wandered round to the delightful English booksellers *Village Voice*, tucked away behind St Sulpice, and bought a copy of *The Da Vinci Code*. I took it home, began to read it and found, to my astonishment, like millions of others before me, that I just could not put the book down. I was immediately inspired to look at reproductions of the paintings in the book. I simply had to verify the descriptions given by the author. In his introduction Dan Brown says, "All descriptions of artwork, architecture, documents and secret rituals in this novel are accurate!" but are they? After all, Brown is a novelist and this is a thriller. This gripping novel certainly raises as many questions as it answers!

I soon found that I could not resist the temptation to check all of these curious observations for myself. I set out to look at the paintings closely, and visit the locations. As a trained historian my first reaction was to go

back to the sources, and see for myself whether there could be any basis for truth in what Brown was telling his readers. The quest was an intriguing trail that led all over Paris. Our guides quickly became specialists in the subject, researching and leading regular tours on this theme. One of our guides is related to the academic Hugh Schonfield who wrote *The Passover Plot*, published in 1967. This book was one of several upon which the controversial subject matter of stories like *The Da Vinci Code* is based.

As my fascination with researching the sources for *The Da Vinci Code* grew, so did the idea of sharing the results. We soon set up a *Da Vinci Code* Tour of Paris, and it wasn't long before it was spotted by editors Constance de Bartillat and Charles Ficat. Their determination, soon "transmogriphied" *The Da Vinci Code* Tour of Paris into the definitive code seekers guide book. As previously stated, many of the ideas in the book are controversial, many of the so-called facts are troubling, they leave plenty of opening for belief but to really find the answers, the only solution is to go on the trail and decide for yourself.

Brown encrypted a four part code on the front cover of his book, offering a trip to Paris for the lucky cryptographer who could decode the message. 40,000 people returned the answers to him! The book, its secrets, codes and conspiracy theory have excited the imaginations of millions. So far, more than a dozen books have been written to help the reader decode Dan Brown's book, which is packed full of codes from cover to cover. These books take diverse points of view. Some are tongue-in-cheek, and others defend Christianity, seeing *The Da Vinci Code* as a threat. One such book, recently published in French, disputed, in a mocking tone, every point made by Brown, offering little analysis and no alternative evidence. The best of them take an intelligent look at the questions raised by the novel, examine its contents and attempt to give a balanced view. This book aims to do this whilst offering a unique way to visit the city of Paris.

Introduction

Chartres

The Blue Virgin of Chartres

IN HIS NOVEL Dan Brown takes us on a journey across Paris that has its origins in our ancient medieval past. Secret societies, the Knights Templars, the Priory of Sion, Masons, and other mysterious groups, used symbols and codes to protect their most precious secrets while passing them on to others. Evidence of this can be found in carvings, sculptures, inscriptions, paintings and objects located in or on the meeting houses of each. In *The Da Vinci Code*, author Brown links these together, sending his hero Langdon on a quest to unravel a code that will lead him to one of the most powerful and carefully kept secrets ever. This guide will take you to those locations and reveal some of their hidden secrets.

Even if you have not read *The Da Vinci Code* you will find this guide book can be enjoyed, and will initiate you into the mysteries and enigmas of Paris. However, if you have read the book, then as you go, you will be able to relive the excitement of the tale as it unfolds and see how some of the intriguing issues raised by Dan Brown relate to the chosen sites and monuments.

This book aims to be a complete manual. It covers the history and background of all the sites mentioned in *The Da Vinci Code*, offering some practical tips as well as containing information about other unusual, mysterious or esoteric monuments and meeting places. We will also unravel some of the puzzles and clues that Brown has woven into his text, for example: The rue Haxo really exists, it is not near Roland-Garros as Brown says, there is no number 24, and there is no Depository Bank of Zurich, but... Haxo is an anagram of Hoax!

Galleries to Golgotha!

The most dramatic events in the book take place in two locations: the magnificent Church of Saint Sulpice, and one of the world's most famous museums, the Louvre. This guide will take you on an in-depth tour of both of these monuments, but this trail, like Langdon's quest, will lead all over the city and even take us out into the countryside to the now famous Château de Villette and the lovely city of Chartres.

Saint Sulpice

Dan Brown's novel has done for St Sulpice what Hugo's *Hunchback of Notre Dame* did for the cathedral of Paris. In the early 19th century the cathedral was in a terribly poor state of repair. As a medieval monument, it was not held in high regard. At this period it was the monuments of the Renaissance that were considered worthy of attention. These were evidence of a *golden age* when at long-last men began to live like civilised beings; they were monuments from an age of enlightenment and learning. Medieval Notre Dame seemed to serve as a reminder of our warrior-like and barbaric past. Hugo's book set both the period and the monument in a completely new light. Literally thousands of visitors came to look at the church again, this time with wonderment at the architectural marvel. The public soon rallied to the cause of preserving what had survived, although they were nearly too late. Medieval windows had been removed to let more light into the church, and the original carved lintel of the central portal had been savagely demolished to allow taller processional banners into the building. The heroic hunchbacked Quasimodo put an end to this destruction!

Hugo's best selling and wonderfully romantic story, like Brown's, also begins by citing a cryptic inscription. Hugo wrote that he had seen this carved into the ancient stones of the cathedral. Had it been left by a mason, or an alchemist? Pilgrims and Quasimodo fans have been coming ever since to seek this curious mark and relive the greatest moments of the famous novel. This is now the case with St Sulpice Church. Visitors come to seek the enigmatic Gnomon beneath which the Priory of Sions' keystone was said to be hidden, and to see where the grisly murder of Sandrine Bieil took place. Hundreds flock to the church who never came before. The church has put articles, clippings and cuttings everywhere, warning the visiting public that it has no real connection with the history or events as told in a recently published novel!

Quasimodo, rue Saint-Julien.

The Louvre

The current curator of the Louvre is apparently not too pleased at being killed off, but is delighted that the museum has found a new crowd of enthusiastic visitors coming to marvel at its magnificent collection of Leonardos. People come to seek coded messages in the *Mona Lisa* and Poussin's *Shepherds of Arcadia*. These can be seen with the aid of this guide, but there is also much more to discover, and the aim of this book is to lead you on your way.

Controversy and criticism

The Da Vinci Code has sparked huge interest world wide, and has sold millions of copies. A simple web search on Google using *Da Vinci Code* + Dan Brown resulted in 1,270,000 hits. But the work has been controversial and the book has been highly criticised from many sides. Religious doctrine, the Holy Grail theory, the supposed relationship between Mary Magdalene and Christ have all come under heavy criticism. These ideas are not at all new. Nikos Kazantzakis, perhaps best known for writing *Zorba the Greek*, evoked the relationship between Christ and Mary Magdalene in *The Last Temptation of Christ* more than 50 years ago! The Roman Catholic Church banned his book, and the Greek Orthodox Church excommunicated him for this work.

Another of the many criticisms levelled at *The Da Vinci Code* is the errors it apparently makes in describing the topography of Paris. As will be illustrated, there are many reasons why Dan Brown describes the city as he does. It is also important to remember that the book is a novel, it has been written to entertain, so let your imagination be entertained as you discover Paris and enter into the fun, like the millions of other people who have thoroughly enjoyed this gripping book. The book is divided into eight main chapters.

CHAPTER HEADINGS

The Seven Seals contains a dictionary of symbols and introduces the main themes and controversies that arise in the book.

Inside the Cryptex decodes the characters and events in the book, explains the meaning of much of the esoteric vocabulary used by Dan Brown, and deciphers some of the codes!

The Lost Statue of Isis examines the Sacred Feminine and where to find her in Paris.

The Paving Stones of Paris leads the way through the city to all the locations that are involved in the story.

Beneath the Rose Line is a complete guided tour of St Sulpice.

Under the Pyramids is a guided *Da Vinci Code* Tour of the Louvre.

Château Villette and Beyond takes you to the places outside Paris that are vital to the story.

The Keystone provides further ideas for those wishing to take the trail one step further, and includes some practical information.

A **full index** makes finding even the lesser known curiosities easy. We hope you find your quest both enjoyable and rewarding!

Saint Denis (Notre-Dame de Paris).

The Seven Seals

Notre Dame

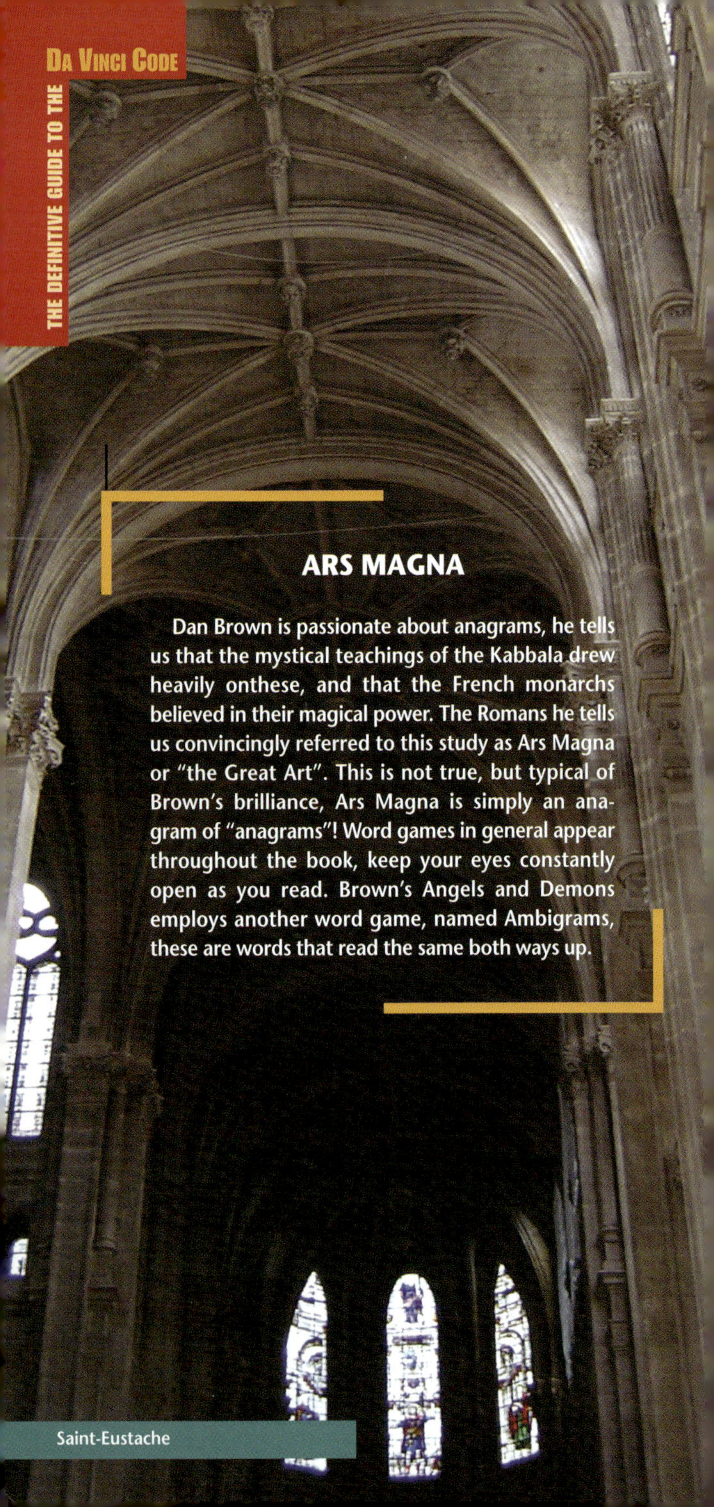

ARS MAGNA

Dan Brown is passionate about anagrams, he tells us that the mystical teachings of the Kabbala drew heavily onthese, and that the French monarchs believed in their magical power. The Romans he tells us convincingly referred to this study as Ars Magna or "the Great Art". This is not true, but typical of Brown's brilliance, Ars Magna is simply an anagram of "anagrams"! Word games in general appear throughout the book, keep your eyes constantly open as you read. Brown's Angels and Demons employs another word game, named Ambigrams, these are words that read the same both ways up.

Saint-Eustache

LANGDON'S DICTIONARY OF SYMBOLS, SACRED AND PROFANE

> *"Let him that hath understanding count the number of the Beast: for it is the number of a man; and his number is 666."*
>
> Book of Revelations 13:18

This section looks at some of the main issues raised in *The Da Vinci Code*, especially the power of symbols. The name "Seven Seals" comes from the last book of the Bible, the Apocalypse or Revelation of John the Divine. The word apocalypse comes from the Greek and means unveiling. This book is a fantastic allegory, evoking strange creatures such as a seven headed monster, plagues of giant locusts and a lamb with seven eyes and ten horns. It is "a coherent symbolic set", as Langdon, the Harvard symbologist would call it! At the beginning of the book, seven seals are broken, and as each seal is unlocked the messages in John's vision are revealed.

The Revelation is an important source of symbols for religious artists, particularly during the early medieval period. Dan Brown's use of the symbols from this book includes the number 666. Symbols are strangely powerful, capable of conveying a strong message. The "Ban the Bomb" sign of the 1960s evokes peace while a skull and cross-bones carries a message of danger.

As with all symbols, the Apocalypse has been adopted and interpreted differently through succeeding ages. The book was written at the end of the 1st century, and refers to the contemporary conditions of Christians under the Roman Empire. The vision described and its symbols, were a thinly disguised or coded criticism of non-Christian powers, especially that of Rome, symbolized by the "Whore of Babylon". The figure of the Beast stood for the pagan Emperor Nero, but its meaning changed through time. Later it came to signify Islam to the crusading Christians, then protestant heresy to the Catholics during the Reformation, and for the Lutherans, it symbolized the corrupt papacy.

The fantastic images from the Revelation, the symbolism of which is often obscure, can be seen in medieval manuscripts, stained-glass windows, frescoes, engravings and tapestries. The best example of this in Paris is the rose window of the **Sainte-Chapelle**, dating from the end of the 15th century. The story is told from the centre of the window outwards, each concentric ring of glass showing the events that take place as each of the seven seals is broken and the book is opened to reveal what lies within.

The following symbols are common in art throughout the ages

666

When Langdon explains the pentagram to Fache, he also explains that the difficulty in deciphering a symbol comes from the fact that it is different for all people. The pentacle in modern culture had become associated with Devil worship, and used as a satanic symbol in horror movies. The same has happened to 666. Dan Brown tells us that 666 is the number of panes of glass in Mitterrand's Pyramid. Originally this number appears in chapter 13 verse 18 of the Revelation of John the Divine, the verse says it is "the number of the beast". This is actually an allusion to Emperor Nero. The study of numeric values in words is known as gematria. Caesar Neron in Greek, when analysed in this manner, equals 666. Greek is used because it is the language of the original book of Revelations. Three consecutive rolls of a dice resulting in 666 are considered to be unlucky, this is often erroneously said to come from the Great Fire of London, although it did take place in 1666. Dan Brown writes that the book of meditations used by Opus Dei consists of 999 maxims. Presumably members are told to keep the book the right way up! In biblical numerology, seven = perfection, there are seven days for Creation and seven days of the week. Six = imperfection, 666 being threefold, forms a trinity of imperfection. The name of Jesus in Greek analysed the same way = 888, and this is interpreted as the number of super-perfection.

Ankh. A cross topped with a loop, the ankh appears frequently in Egyptian art. Its original meaning is still debated but its hieroglyphic meaning is "life". For this reason it is a frequent attribute of the gods and is often shown being handed to the king. As a symbol it points to divine and eternal life. The ankh was adopted by the Coptic Church (Christian Church in

Egypt) and called the *Crux Ansata*. Saunière has added a collection of ankhs to the Louvre because of its association with the Goddess and life giving (➤ **See the Louvre chapter in this book**).

Apples. A very important symbol in *The Da Vinci Code*, the word apple opens the final cryptex. In Christian images the apple is the fruit of the tree of knowledge and symbolises the fall of Eve. This symbol descends fom Greek mythology. The daughters of Atlas guarded the golden fruit of an apple tree with the help of a snake, but Hercules stole the apples. In mythology, Paris, the Trojan prince, awards a golden apple to Venus. This gift causes the Trojan war. Apples are also the attributes of the three Graces, the handmaidens of Venus (➤ **See Venus in the Louvre chapter**). When shown held by the infant Christ the fruit symbolises his role as redeemer.

Baphomet. This figure is really the key to *The Da Vinci Code*. Baphomet is represented as a human figure with wings and horns, like a rebel angel. Under torture, the Templars admitted to worshiping him. The biblical scholar Hugh Schonfield applied the Atbash Cipher to the name and found that once decoded, it revealed the word Sophia, which means wisdom in Greek. Sophia is also the Goddess considered to be the bride of God (➤ **See Shekinah p. 143**). From this it is argued that the Templars were worshipers and protectors of the Sacred Feminine. A sculpture of Baphomet can be seen crowning the portal of the Church of St Merry.

Blade and Chalice. The two symbols (Λ V) represent respectively the phallus or male, and the womb or the feminine. They are alluded to throughout *The Da Vinci Code*. One placed above the other makes a sacred union of male and female, and forms the hourglass shape of the Holy Grail. The Grail itself symbolises union, the womb and the bloodline. Superimposed on top of each other blade and chalice make a star of David. This is also the shape of I. M. Pei's inverted pyramid complex at the Louvre, a fact exploited to wonderful effect by Dan Brown.

Caduceus. This is the staff of Mercury. It is intertwined with two snakes and topped with wings. The staff was used by Mercury to separate two fighting serpents and therefore symbolises peace. The symbol is used by the medical and business world. This is due to an ancient belief in the healing powers of snake venim, and the fact that peace is always good

for business. There is also a link between the words mercantile/merchants and the name Mercury.

Chi-rho. This monogram can be seen in most churches, and consists of the Greek letters chi and rho, the first two letters of Christ's name. It is commonly found in Christian art from the 4th century, often between the symbols AΩ, alpha and omega. It was originally used in pre-Christian times when it was a symbol of good omen (the letters are an abreviation of the Greek word *chrestos* meaning "auspicious"). The symbol was adopted by Emperor Constantine for the Imperial Roman standard, probably for pagan rather than Christian reasons. This sign appeared in a dream to Constantine before his battle with Maxentius.

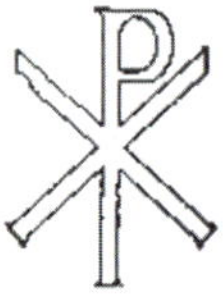

Fish. A symbol of both Christ and baptism. The Greek word for fish IXθYΣ forms the initials of Jesus/Christ/of God/the Son/Saviour. In the 1st and 2nd centuries, believers were called "pisciculi" or little fishes and the baptismal font "piscina" literally a fish pond. The font is often octagonal or eight-sided, seven is the number of man, one the number of God, the total of eight which equals perfection.

Fleur de Lys. The white lily symbolises purety, and it has been used by the French monarchs since the 12th century. The fleur de lys, formed like the pointed end of a lance, also represents military force. The lily as a symbol of purety frequently appears in paintings of the Annunciation.

Greek Cross. Cross with four arms of equal length.

Holy Grail. According to legend, it is the vessel used by Jesus at the Last Supper, and later by Joseph of Arimathea to collect and preserve the blood of Christ after the Crucifixion. The miraculous vessel pre-dates Christianity and is a feminine symbol representing the womb in which life-giving transformation occurs. The vessel or vase was central to alchemical tradition in ancient China and this reached Northern Europe in the 12th century. Medieval mystics saw it as a representation of the soul, to be filled and replenished with divine grace. *The Da Vinci Code* theory that the Grail is the relics of Mary Magdalene, giver of life, is based upon this interpretation. In the book, the Grail consists of an actual tomb, physical relics, and documents relating to Mary Magdalene. Saint Graal means Holy Cup or Chalice, but is also interpreted as Sang Real or Royal Blood.

IHS. Abbreviation of the name Jesus in Latin.

INRI. Latin inscription pinned on the Cross at the Crucifixion, written by Pilate to mock Christ: Iesus Nazarenus Rex Iudaeorum – Jesus of Nazareth, King of the Jews. These initials are often shown on the Cross in paintings or sculptures of the Crucifixion.

Lamb. Symbol of sacrifice, for a full explanation ➤ See p. 148.

Olympic Rings. Langdon attributes esoteric origins to the Olympic rings, linking them to the eight year cycle of the planet Venus around which the original games were organised. According to the Olympic Charter, the five rings were chosen by Pierre de Coubertin in 1913 to symbolise the union of 5 continents. The games were held every four years and this period is called an Olympiad. The first Olympic games in Paris were in 1900, the 2nd in 1924.

Pelican. A myth said that the pelican would pluck flesh from her own breast to feed her young. This led to the bird becoming a symbol of sacrifice and therefore of the Crucifixion. A beautifully sculpted example of this can be seen on the roof of the sacristy at the back end of St Sulpice Church.

Pentacle. An ancient pagan symbol in the form of a five pointed star. Langdon says it is associated with Devil worship, but it actually represents the Sacred Feminine or Divine Goddess. It is a symbol of Venus because the planet supposedly traces a pentacle in the sky. The pentacle symbolises perfection and beauty because the sections it creates correspond to the Golden Mean. In Chrisitan iconography it has been used to symbolise the five wounds of Christ. For Pythagoras the pentacle was the symbol of man, encompasing the five points (head and limbs) of *the Vitruvian Man*. It also corresponds to the five elements from which man was believed to be made up: earth, water, fire, air and psyche or plasma.

Rose. Teabing says the rose is the Priory symbol for the Grail which is in effect Mary Magdalene. It is linked to the pentacle by its five petaled form and is also the anagram of Eros, god of sexual love. The rose was brought back from the Holy Lands by the Crusaders and became a sign of romantic love; it was adopted by the neo-platonists and evolved first as a symbol of pure love, then as symbol of the Virgin Mary. The rose windows on cathedrals dedicated to Notre Dame are symbols of this. The Virgin Mary can be seen standing in front of the central rose on the west façade of Notre Dame in Paris. The rose was sacred to Venus in Antiquity, and is her attribute in Renaissance and later art, at which time the pricking of its thorns was associated with the wounds of love.

Snake. The Red Snake of the "Secret Dossiers" symbolises the blood line of Christ. In Christian iconography the serpent represents evil or Satan, but for the ancients the snake symbolised fertility, wisdom and the power to heal. In the Lady Chapel at St Sulpice, the Virgin, sculpted by Pigalle, is treading on the serpent, symbolising the vanquishing of sin. The snake is also the symbol of prudence ("Be wary as serpents", Matthew 10:16).

Swastika. Perhaps no better example exists of the power of symbols. The swastika is extremely ancient. It can be drawn both left and right facing. This symbol had universally positive connotations until the rise of Fascism. It was used by Hindus to symbolise universal stability. In Buddhism it is called *Manji* and represents universal harmony. In Jaïnism it is an auspicious symbol. Until the rise of Fascism, Rudyard Kipling incorporated a swastika in his bookcovers symbolising his interest in Indian culture. Many companies used this emblem as a logo: the Finnish Air Force and Army, the Swedish company AESA, even the boy scouts in Britain. Once adopted by Nazi Germany, the symbol became synonymous with terror. This corruption of an ancient and powerful symbol has lead to it becoming taboo in modern times.

How symbols change over time

Star of David or Solomon's Seal. Two interlocking triangles, the blade and chalice once again. The six pointed star is recognised today as the universal symbol of the Jewish people. The symbol is however extremely ancient and was used by occult groups before taking on its modern symbolism. Some Orthodox Jewish groups reject its use because of its association with magic and the occult. It is an important astrological symbol in Zoroastrianism. The first mention of it in rabbinic literature is in the mid 12th century. Jewish lore suggests that either King David had this emblem on his shield or that his shield was this shape, and it is thus a symbol of protection. Proof of the power of symbols as described by Langdon, and particularly of their adoption and shifting meaning, is the yellow star that Jews were made to wear during the Holocaust. This was extended to all Jews over the age of six in German occupied areas on the 6th of September 1941. Triangular badges that were colour coded were forced upon other groups too. The Nazis obliged homosexuals to wear a pink triangle. This illustrates the organic nature of the symbol. The pink triangle is today internationally recognized as identifying the gay community. Various badges are exhibited at the beautiful and poignant **Monument to the Deported in the square de l'Île-de-France, behind Notre Dame.** ➤ **See also the synagogue by Hector Guimard, rue Pavé, and the Renaissance chapel of the École des Beaux-Arts, rue Bonaparte, 75006.**

An Alchemical Distillation

Some of the main issues raised in *The Da Vinci Code*

Many books which have been written about *The Da Vinci Code* violently attack its content and debunk the theories developed. These have mostly been written by Christian groups or authors. This has the adverse affect of adding fuel to the fire as it reinforces the idea that there really is something to hide.

However, many of the main issues raised by Dan Brown have caused contention. The theories upheld by his heros are based on a wide range of research. The following four books develop the main issues in depth. If you wish to do some further reading, these are good places to start.

The Holy Blood and The Holy Grail. Baigent Leigh and Lincoln. Arrow Books, 1982.

The Templar Revelation. Picknet and Prince. Touchstone, 1998.

The Woman with the Alabaster Jar. Margaret Starbird. Bear and Company, 1993.

The Passover Plot. Hugh Schonfield. Element books Ltd, re-issue 1998.

The Code Book. Simon Singh. Anchor books, 1999.

A Great Treasure

Somewhere in Europe a great treasure is hidden. Its exact content is not known, nor are the identities of those who hid it, or keep it hidden. The Temple in Jerusalem was sacked by the Romans in 70 AD and the contents of the Holy of Holies was taken back to Rome. This treasure may have included the Ark of the Covenant. The great treasure may also have been that of the Merovingian kings, or that of Margaret of Provence. She carried a fortune with her to pay the ransom wanted for her husband, Saint Louis, but on learning of his death, she is said to have hidden it.

The Cathars were also purported to have kept something of extraordinary value which was probably sacred. This could have been hidden or passed onto the Templars at the time of the Albigensian Crusades, as many high ranking Templars were of Cathar families. Later on the Freemasons appropriated the Templars as their antecedents, and may have become guardians of the treasure. Sion is the symbol of the Temple, and it is argued that the "Priory of Sion", became the keepers of the secret. The question asked is whether this could be the treasure that real life Saunière found at Rennes-le-Château?

Wedding Vows

It is argued that the above mentioned treasure is more than wealth, that it is a sacred symbol of the marriage of Christ and Mary Magdalene. A symbol that could prove that the divinity of Christ was invented by man, and that Christ fathered a line of descendants who became the Merovingians. The association of Mary Magdalene with France is alluded to in the account of her life in *The Golden Legend*. What are believed to be her relics, including a skull, are kept at the Basilique St Marie-Madeleine at St Maximin in Provence.

Some of the main arguments put forward to support the theory of Christ's marriage come from the New Testament, others from the Gnostic Gospels. It is said that it would have been very unusual for Christ not to be married and that if he was not, it would have been mentioned in the Bible. Mary Magdalene anoints Christ with spikenard. This is an ointment which was used at wedding ceremonies, and it was apparently used by Mary Magdalene to anoint Christ at the Wedding of Cana. It is said that this event probably represents their own marriage. Jesus did not preach celibacy, Matthew 19:4-5.

Mary Magdalene is with Christ at the most crucial moments of his life, including the Crucifixion, and his burial. She is the first to see him after the Resurrection.

Other arguments are:

Jesus treated women as equals, but later writers of the Epistles contributed to the suppression of the role of women. In the Nag Hammadi text known as the Gospel of Mary we learn of the disbelief of Andrew concerning Mary Magdalene seeing Christ resurrected, and we read of Peter's jealousy over Mary Magdalene.

Jesus treats women in an extraordinary way. For example, he ignores the ritual impurity laws in Mark 5:25-34, and refers to women as "daughters of Abraham" in Luke 13:16. In Luke 7:35 Jesus refers to both women and men as children of wisdom and in Luke 8:1-3 he demonstrates that women were part of his inner circle. He talked to foreign women in John 4:7, and he taught women in Luke 10:38-42, when he teaches Martha for example. These are just a few of the arguments put forward in the above books, for more information read the chapter entitled Isis.

Gnostics

Dan Brown evokes the Gnostics. Little was known about Gnosticism until the discovery of the Nag Hammadi texts in the mid 20th century. This system of religious belief was prominent by the 2nd century but seen as heretic by the early Church. One of the Gnostic Gospels most often referred to is the gospel of Thomas which describes Christ and Sophia as aspects of God that make up the complete God known as the Pleroma. There is another important text known as the Pistis Sophia, which links Sophia to Mary Magdalene, and there is a Gnostic Gospel of Mary that proclaims the pre-eminence of Mary Magdalene, whom the Gnostics are believed to have venerated in the form of the Sacred Feminine. The Cathars and the Templars are said to have maintained this tradition, becoming the guardians of her sacred relics.

A Barrow Full of Books

Abigail and Penelope run the well stocked English language bookstore *The Red Wheel Barrow* at 22 rue St Paul. The previously listed book titles can be bought or ordered from them. The shop is located in the heart of the old Marais Quarter near metro St Paul. Penelope and Abigail's names are decoded for you. You can ask them to decode the name of their shop.

Abigail. A Hebrew name meaning "a fathers joy". In the first book of Samuel, Abigail is "a woman of good understanding and of a beautiful countenance." In the play *The Scornful Lady*, by Shakespeare's contemporaries, Beaumont and Fletcher, Abigail is the heroine's confidential helper. As a result, Abigail came to mean any confidential attendant. After the Reformation many Old Testament names became popular in England.

Penelope. The wife of Ulysses, ruler of Ithaca. Whilst Ulysses was absent fighting the Trojan wars, Penelope had many suitors, who tried to convince her that her husband would never return. To delay the suitors Penelope agreed that she would make her choice once the cloth she was weaving was finished. Each night she unravelled her work and began again. The suitors took up residence in her home and held riotous parties, but when Ulysses returned, he slew them, and with Penelope, once again, ruled over Ithaca. The name became widespread in the 17th century. According to old Welsh tales Penelope is a "fairy name".

Inside the Cryptex

Saint-Eustache

Cluny Museum

THE CRYPTEX™ is a design of genius. Historically it does not appear to have actually existed although the Ancients had many ingenious ways to protect secrets including both the use of codes and lockable devices. As early as the 5th century BC, the Greeks used a form of cryptex called the Spartan Scytale. It consisted of a message written on a long band, which could only be read if it was wound around the correct sized baton, allowing the letters to align into a coherent text. One of the recent books written about *The Da Vinci Code* criticizes Brown by arguing that there is no way the cryptex would work, saying that the vinegar in the internal phial could not possibly dissolve papyrus. This may be true, but it is likely that the vinegar would make a terrible mess of the ink! There seems to be no evidence that Leonardo invented the device, it seems to be a true creation of Brown's. The concept and the name are brilliant. Cryptex appears in no dictionary (yet!) and is therefore a neologism, very probably of Brown's own invention. Now the conundrum: if it does not really exist, how come there is a photo! Well it seems that the real Leonardo behind the cryptex is Justin Nevins. You can see, and even order, his beautiful work at *www.cryptex.org*. He hand-makes these

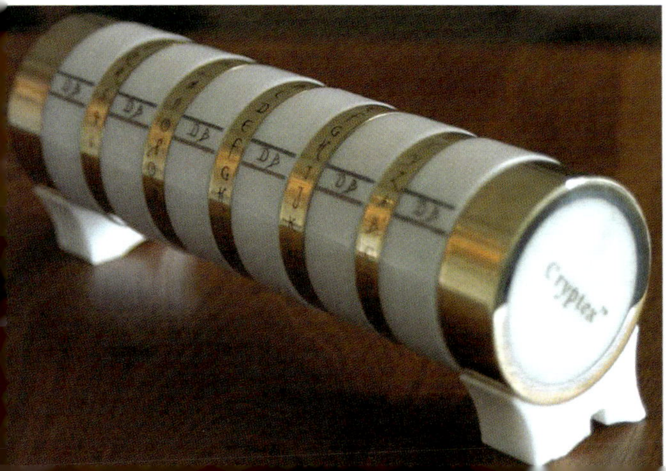

objects according to his own design and his customer's specifications. In a recent interview I asked him how he acquired the secret. He replied that it had been handed down to him by a Grand Master of the Priory of Sion! Each one takes him four to six weeks to make, and can be made from a variety of different materials including metal, stone and beautiful wood. Justin has been fascinated by games and puzzles since he was a child, and creating the cryptex was obviously an irresistible challenge for him. So far he has made about 100. His favourites are not necessarily the ones that use the most precious materials, but the ones that incorporate his client's most ingenious and personal clues. Set yourself the challenge, work out your code, and order your cryptex!

Sophie's World

The *Who's Who* of *The Da Vinci Code,* the cast of characters and their guide to Paris

Dan Brown has presented his readers with a cast of colourful characters that some literary critics have called shallow and trite. A careful look at their character traits, every personal detail and their names, reveals to the Joycean web woven by Brown. The description of each character is completed with suggestions of what they might have done in Paris.

Sandrine Bieil

Here we find two names linked with the quest for the Holy Grail. The abbé Bieil was the Director General of the Seminary of St Sulpice when the real life Saunière of Rennes-le-Château brought the mysterious documents he discovered to the church. Gino Sandri, from whom Brown takes the name Sandrine, was the personal secretary of Pierre Plantard, the Grand Master of the Priory of Sion, in modern times. The nun, guardian of the keystone, is murdered in the church by Silas. **Living in the church she would have done her shopping at the lovely nearby covered market – The Marché St Germain, and probably bought home-**

made produce (jams, biscuits, incense, essential oils) from the monastery shop of Paris.

- **Marché St Germain, 75006, (food shops, boutiques and restaurants) metro Odéon or Mabillon. Monastic Produce, boutique of the Fraternité monastique de Jérusalem, 10, rue des Barres, 75004, metro Hotel-de-Ville.**
- **Shops specializing in devotional objects are located all around St Sulpice, especially rue du Vieux-Colombier.**

Bishop Aringarosa

The Opus Dei Cardinal is devoted to saving his church by obtaining the Grail before anyone else. He is well meaning but has been duped. He is mortified at the deaths caused by his efforts, and ever forgiving. He is the patron of Silas, as Frollot is the patron of Quasimodo in another thriller set in Paris! At first we are led to believe he is the villain, but his Italian name "aringa" and "rosa" means red herring. There is a hidden rose in his name, and his Christian name Manuel means guide or handbook.

Aringarosa's favourites:

- **Shrine of St Vincent de Paul. This saint was associated with the Compagnie du St Sacrement at St Sulpice. The saint's body is preserved in a spectacular glass reliquary case and can be seen at the chapelle des prêtres de la Mission lazariste, 95, rue de Sèvres, 75006 (metro Vaneau).**
- **He would also worship at the Church of the Miraculous Medal, rue du Bac, 75007 (metro Sèvres-Babylone).**
- **The extraordinary tomb of Richelieu in the Chapel of the Sorbonne would fascinate him. Richelieu is shown in the act of dropping down dead, supported by two muses, with his enormous Cardinal's hat hovering above the sepulchre. Chapel of the Sorbonne, place de la Sorbonne, 75005 (metro Cluny).**

Collet

The assistant to Fache. He follows the trail through the book but always seems to be one step behind. Although, his name in French means "a noose" or "to snare". Collet is made to feel rather uncomfortable, alone at night in Saunière's office, being stared at by the metre tall model knight in armour. A cure for his phobia – a visit to the armour galleries at the superb ➤ **Military Museum, les Invalides, 75007 (which includes Napoleon's Tomb). Metro Varenne or Invalides. Open every day, 10am-5pm.**

La Sorbonne

(Captain) Fache Bézu

He carries himself like an angry ox, he is therefore "Le Taureau" (the bull). Fache is deeply religious and later shows great compassion to Aringarosa. He is described in chapter 4 as having "hair slicked back with an arrow-like widow's peak, preceding him like the prow of a ship." The arrow is the sign of the male, the prow of a ship is the symbol of Paris. Fache evoques the French word for anger, and Bézu is a mysterious mountain close to Rennes-le-Château, associated with the Templars. The captain is part of the Direction centrale de police judiciaire (DCPJ), which is an equivalent of the FBI.

Bézu's favourites:

- **The Police Museum, a wonderful collection of documents and objects that evoke famous crimes and mysteries including the blade of the guillotine used at the Revolution. The Police Museum, 4, rue de la Montagne-St-Geneviève, 75005. Metro Maubert-Mutualité. 9am-5pm, closed Sundays (free).**

Jonas Faukman

Another subtle anagram. Jason Kaufman is Dan Brown's real editor. Jonas plays a minor, but key role and has the most telling line in the book. It is he that sent Langdon's book to Saunière for approval, setting in motion the "Langdon-commits-murder" connection. When Langdon presents his manuscript "Symbols of the lost Sacred Feminine" to his publisher, Faukman says, "You're a Harvard historian, for God's sake, not a pop schlock-meister looking for a quick buck." Is this Brown's conscience speaking? Apparently Kaufman negotiated a two book deal for Brown worth half a million dollars. **In Paris, any editor would stroll along the rue Servandoni, make a pilgrimage to one of Paris' most literary streets, rue de l'Odéon and admire the windows of the city's editors, ancient book shops and charming old world bookbinders. This is where Sylvia Beach had her famous bookshop *Shakespeare and Company*. The world of editors has been in the Latin Quarter since the Sorbonne obtained its first printing press in late medieval times.**

Claude Grouard

Is the security warden at the Louvre, forced to release Sophie and Langdon when she takes a Caravaggio hostage.

He was very fond of his boss Saunière. An adoring security agent whose name is an anagram of ardour and cudgel! **Favourites in Paris: days when the Louvre is on strike!**

Robert Langdon

Harvard Symbologist. (The expression does not exist but will undoubtedly enter the English language soon.) Real life John Langdon seemingly invented the Ambigram which is a word that reads the same upside-down or the right way up. Some examples can be seen at *www.johnlangdon.net.* A Scottish gardener called Charles Jencks has created a garden around this theme. Langdon is past middle age, brilliant, attractive and a specialist in the symbols of the Sacred Feminine. Lang is like language, and don is a university lecturer. His name makes the anagram "Art golden born".

Langdon's favourites would be:

- **The National Archives Museum, 87, rue Vieille-du-Temple.**
- **Cabinet of Antiquities. Bibliothèque nationale, 58, rue de Richelieu, 75002, metro Bourse or Pyramides (free).**
- **Bibliothèque nationale de France-François-Mitterrand, 11, quai François-Mauriac, 75013, metro Bibliothèque François-Mitterrand. (Fantastic modern architecture, four towers symbolizing open books around a sunken pine forest.)**

Having experienced being trapped in a Dali painting, he'd try the

- **Dali Museum, espace Dali, 11, rue Poulbot, 75018, metro Abbesses. Open every day 10am-6.30pm.**

Rémy Legaludec

Rémy is the cool but over ambitious manservant of Teabing. He does all the "Teacher's" dirty work and is then killed off thanks to the Teacher's knowledge of his allergy to nuts. He attempts to save the day several times but is mercilessly murdered. His name is an anagram of his two functions in the story: A cudgel merely, and allergy! There is a beautiful park in the 13th arrondisement called square René-Le Gall, the trees of which follow the banks of the ancient Bievre River. In amongst the obelisks and pergolas, it is perfect for a pic-nic. Next door is the maternity clinic, the Villa Isis! The Observatory of Paris, the starting point of the Rose Line can be seen at nearby metro Port-Royal.

Legaludec's bugging skills would have led him to the

➤ **Musée de la Radio, Radio France, 116, avenue du Président-Kennedy, 75016, metro Ranelagh. Closed weekends, must reserve 01 56 40 21 80.**

Bérenger Saunière

This non fictional character was the poor parish priest at the heart of the Grail mystery evoked in the book *The Holy Blood and The Holy Grail*, by Baigent, Lee and Lincoln. His life story is a tangle of confusing leads that has caused furore amongst researchers and is the catalyst for *The Da Vinci Code*. His sudden and extravagant spending aroused the suspicions of local ecclesiastics. He was accused of illicitly selling masses and was suspended from his post. Saunière appealed to the Vatican, his suspension was overruled and he was reinstated. He was obviously a man of great influence! He died on January the 17th 1917, the feast day of St Sulpice. 17th January is also inscribed on one of the tombstones in his churchyard. The inscription on the same tombstone was a coded message containing references to Poussin and Teniers as a key to the same message that Saunière found hidden in his church. He had the tombstone inscription removed, not knowing it had previously been copied. ➤ **To further your quest, see Poussin in the Louvre section.**

Saunière's Favourites:

➤ **Extravagant shopping spree at Galeries Lafayette and Printemps, department stores behind the Opera, metro Havre-Caumartin, and who knows, perhaps the Museum of Forgeries "Contrefaçon" 16, rue de la Faisanderie, 75016, metro Porte Dauphine.**

Jacques Saunière

Saunière takes his family name from the priest at Rennes-le-Château and his Christian name from Jacques de Molay. In the book he is curator of the Louvre, Grand Master of the Priory of Sion, grandfather of Sophie Neveu, specialist of Goddess Symbols and guardian of the Grail. A busy man who still found time to practise Hieros Gamos! Look in the Louvre chapter to rediscover the incredible message he has time to leave before expiring in the Louvre. **As Jacques is dead, go and visit the Cemetery of Père-**

Lachaise, metro Père-Lachaise. Tombs of the famous and infamous, beautiful and macabre. Open every day. Look out for the tomb of Allan Kardec, founder of spiritism. It is a copy of a pre-historic pagan burial monument, and one of the most visited tombs in this graveyard.

Silas

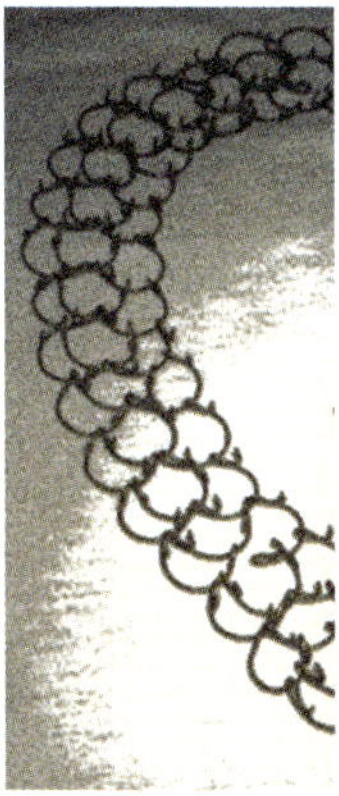

A "hulking albino" who like Quasimodo was adopted by a church superior. His loyalty to Opus Dei pushed him to commit a pentacle of five murders. His name is that of a Bible character whose story is told in Acts chapter 15 and 16, notably in 16:26. He is one of Paul's main missionary companions. Biblical Silas is released from prison with Paul after an earthquake destroys the building. In Acts 15:41 he "confirms the churches of Cilicia." His own name evokes both Cilicia, and the cilice belt that he wears. **Visit rue La Bruyère in the 9th arrondisement to look for the house where Silas takes a much needed rest after murdering Sandrine Bieil. Can't find Opus Dei? Then visit the nearby Gustave Moreau Museum to see mysterious symbolist paintings, or the Museum of Romantic Life for souvenirs of George Sand, Chopin and 19th century bohemian life.**

- **Musée Gustave-Moreau, 14, rue de La Rochefoucauld, 75009, metro Trinité. Closed Tuesdays, 10am-12pm, 2pm-5pm.**
- **Musée de la Vie romantique, 16, rue Chaptal, 75009, metro Trinité. Closed Mondays, 10am-6pm.**

Sophie Neveu

A name containing appropriate clues including the initials of the Priory of Sion. Neveu is close to the French word for "new" and Eve can be found in her name. Is she the new Eve? Her name can be made into anagram of "Oh, Supine Eve". This would evoke the fallen woman having been forced to become submissive. In Greek, Sofia means wisdom and also contains the syllable phi, the name of the golden section. The Gnostics consider Sofia as the mystical consort of Christ. This belief is based on a Nag Hammadi text known as Sofia (Wisdom) of Christ. Is Sophie Neveu herself a Grail,

carrying the bloodline of Christ? Dan Brown, hints at this but chooses not to resolve the question. The name is sheer cryptic brilliance, hats off to Dan Brown! The French version of "Friends reunited" website, "Copains d'avant", has registered 10,081 Neveus in France but surprisingly not one Bézu!
Sophie is an attractive but unusually unfashionable Parisian, in "sweater, leggings and hair falling unstyled to her shoulders". She probably does her shopping at the wonderful flea market at Porte de Clignancourt.

Why not invite her to

➤ **Paris' museum of fashion, palais Galliera, avenue du Président-Wilson, 75016, metro Iéna or Pont de l'Alma.**

The Flame of Liberty, which stands nearby, at Alma Bridge has become the unofficial monument to a modern female idol, Lady Diana.

Leigh Teabing

A man of knowledge who could teach us a thing or two! Leigh Teabing, what a hotchpotch! Quintessential English gent, hence the Tea! Teabing is an anagram of one of the authors of *The Holy Blood and The Holy Grail*, and Leigh the second author's name. The third contributor Lincoln is alluded to in the life of Teabing, notably in his role of making T.V. programmes. At first he is presented as a charming rascal and then he is shown as a villain. Could this be a reflection of Brown's own opinion of their book. Teabing is also exceedingly rich. I'm still perplexed by the leg irons, any suggestions to *bartillat@wanadoo.fr*. Teabing could be found ambling through the lovely old covered arcades of Paris looking for ancient papers, documents, parchments and statuettes for his mantelpiece.

His favourite boutique is probably the tiny shop specializing in collectable walking sticks, just inside passage Jouffroy.

➤ **M.G. Segas, 34, passage Jouffroy, 75009.**

➤ **Passage des Panoramas, passage Jouffroy, and passage Verdeau, 75002 and 75009. Metro Grands-Boulevards.**

➤ **Museum of Letters and Manuscripts, 8, rue de Nesle, 75006, metro Odéon or Pont-Neuf. Thursday to Sunday, 10am-6pm.**

➤ **Louvre des antiquaires, place du Palais-Royal, 75001.**

➤ **Also, Angelina's, a famous tearoom with beautiful patisseries, although you won't find the scones that Teabing serves his late night visitors.**

Pamela Gettum

Irresistable Pamela! Welcoming, warm, smiling and efficient. The name Pamela is another of Brown's sharp Greek references! It was coined by Philip Sidney in the 1580s in his romance *Arcadia* (is this a reference to Poussin again?). Sidney combined Pan, meaning all, with meli, meaning honey; our librarian is certainly all honey. The imagery in her chapter (92) is almost Shakespearean: eyes are everywhere, perfect for a library. Pamela wears thick horn-rimmed glasses, she winks twice in three sentences, she eyes bits of paper, she shoots quick glances, and she also makes tea for weary researchers. As for Gettum, need I say more?

Her favourites in Paris:

The English Language Bookstores:

- **The Red Wheelbarrow, 22, rue St Paul, 75004, metro St Paul.**
- **Village Voice, 6, rue Princesse, 75006, metro Mabillon (around the corner from St-Sulpice).**
- **San Francisco Bookstore, 17, rue Monsieur-le-Prince, 75006, metro Mabillon or Odéon.**
- **Tea and Tattered Pages, 24, rue Mayet, 75006, metro Duroc.**
- **And of course the Museum of Lorgnettes and Spectacles, 85, rue du Faubourg-St-Honoré, 75008, metro Concorde: 10am-12pm, 2pm-6pm.**

Vernet André

André Vernet is the manager of the Depository Bank of Zurich, and therefore indirectly the protector of the keystone. He is an old friend of Saunière and of course his initials A + V symbolize blade and chalice! Dan Brown doesn't miss a chance. The name also appears in the many acknowledgements Brown makes in his book. As he is the protector of a great treasure, he is perhaps Brown's contented bank manager?! If this is the case, his favourite in Paris would be:

- **The Museum of Money, "La Monnaie" 11, quai Conti, 75006, metro Pont-Neuf (The history of money, fabrication of coins and medals and a collection of coins through the ages.)**

Detail from the gnomon, St-Sulpice

The Da Vinci Code Glossary

Alchemist/Alchemy. ➤ See under Nicolas Flamel's house, and Philosopher's Stone p. 107.

Amon. Egyptian god, his name means the hidden one, he was thought of as the power behind the sun. His headdress consists of a sun disk and feathers symbolising truth. He is a god of fertility. Therefore, his symbols are the ram's horns and the snake. The spiral amonite shell is named after Amon's spiraling horns.

Apocrypha. Greek word meaning hidden things. This expression was originally applied to any writing restricted to members of a secret society or sect. Among Christians it was applied to texts not included in the Bible. There are two categories of apocrypha: the books not found in the Hebrew Old Testament but included in the Septuagint, (the pre-christian Greek translation of the Hebrew) and the 40 or so books relating to Old and New Testament characters that have been denied scriptural authority and don't appear in the Christian Bible. Many Christian images are drawn from these books, see Heliodorus in St Sulpice.

Arago Plaques. These medallions give physical form to an abstract idea, marking out the meridian of Paris. ➤ See full description on p. 128.

Armour. Was worn by knights and noblemen. The privileges of nobility came at a price, that of protecting them for king and country in times of war. The history of armour can be traced from Homeric times to the 19th century at the Invalides Museum.

Cathars. A Christian sect who refused to acknowledge the authority of the pope. They believed the cross was a symbol of human torture, and disapproved of the lucrative trade of holy relics. They believed in the marriage of Christ and Mary Magdalene. The Cathars were persecuted by the Inquisition between 1209 and 1255, they had been virtually anihilated. Little evidence of their beliefs has survived except the biased information gathered by the Inquisition. They are supposed to have hidden a great treasure, and it is suggested that this may be what Saunière found at Rennes-le-Château.

Cilice Belt. The cilice belt is a spiked band worn by certain members of Opus Dei as part of the practice known as corporal mortification. Silas wears one around his thigh. Teabing knowing this is able to aim for his "weak-spot" during the moment of danger when Silas is about to steal the Keystone. In Latin, the *cilicium* is a covering made of Cilician goat's hair (a horse or goat's hair shirt was worn under fine clothing as a penance). ➤ **See also Discipline.**

Clovis. The first Christian king of France, he was baptised at Reims on Christmas Day 496. This began the tradition of kings being crowned there. Clovis was a Merovingian, the dynastic name comes from his grandfather Merovaeus. He died in his capital, Paris, in 511. His tomb can now be seen at the Basilica of St Denis.

Constantine. † 337. After a vision and a military victory that he attributed to divine intervention, he converted to Christianity. He founded the Christian city of Constantinople, and was one of the first builders of churches including the Holy Sepulchre in Jerusalem. Constantine sent his mother Helena on a pilgrimage to seek the relics of Christ, this story is told in a window at Sainte-Chapelle, ➤ **See p. 101**. St Helena, a latecomer to Christianity is the patron saint of people who are never on time! Constantine was baptised just before he died.

Council of Nicaea. 1st ecumenical council of the Church, took place at Niceae in 325 AD, now Iznik in Turkey. The action taken at this council forms the core of *The Da Vinci Code*. Issues decided upon included the doctrine of the Holy Trinity and the divinity of Christ. The Creed of Niceae proclaimed that Jesus and God were of the same substance,

Hôtel de Sully

Credo = belief. The Creed was modified at a second council in 381. This is the Nicene Creed recited during Catholic mass today.

Crux Ansata. This is the hooped cross used by the Coptic Church. It has the same form as the Egyptian ankh.

Crux Gemmata. A jewel incrusted crucifix, worn by Fache in *The Da Vinci Code*. Beautiful Wisigothic examples can be seen in the Cluny Museum, suspended beneath golden votive crowns (room 16).

Dagobert. Frankish king of Merovingian Dynasty † 639. Dagobert's tomb is visible at St Denis Basilica.

Discipline. Knotted rope used for "mortification of the flesh" by Silas in *The Da Vinci Code*. It has been used since ancient times as has the wearing of a horse hair shirt. (➤ See Pascal p. 123) Certain Opus Dei members (numeraries) use this on themselves once a week. They are encouraged to request permission to do so more often. Other forms of corporal mortification practised by Opus Dei include sleeping on the floor, no pillow, fasting, long silences and cold showers. The philosophy behind this is to "Chasten the body and reduce it to servitude." "Blessed be pain, loved be pain, sanctified be pain, glorified be pain" *(The Way 208)*.

Dossiers Secrets. This is the title of documents pertaining to the Priory of Sion, including the Serpent Rouge. The texts were allegedly written by Henry Lobineau. Lobineau is strangely the name of the street just behind St Sulpice. It is claimed that the Dossier was deposited in the Bibliothèque nationale on the 17th of January 1967. This is the saint's day of St Sulpice.

Et Tu Robert? Question sent to Langdon by Catholic Bishop of Philadelphia after his T.V. appearance defending his Grail theory. This echoes what Caesar said to Brutus, "Et Tu Brutus?" meaning "even you Brutus?". He says this when he realises that Brutus is about to murder him. In *Da Vinci Code* p. 295, from Shakespeare's *Julius Caesar*.

Friday the 13th. Date of round up and arrest of the Knights Templars and therefore, nowadays, associated with bad luck.

Gargoyles. The drains of churches and cathedrals, usually carved into fantastic creatures. Their name comes from the gurgling of water. Marvellous examples at Notre Dame, St Merry, St Severin and many other churches in Paris.

Goddess Worship. Goddess Worship and its surpression is a main theme of *The Da Vinci Code*. ➤ **See chapter Isis.**

Golden Legend. This is an encyclopedia of the lives of the saints, written by a medieval monk Jacques de Voragine, sometime before 1264. This book became a reference for artists, and the iconography of saint's lives is frequently based on these tales (see the two references to Mary the Egyptian, and the church and fountain of St Julian the Poor).

Hermes Trismegystus. Was the teacher of a magical system known as Hermetism. High magic and alchemy were part of the schooling. Trismegystus means three times great.

Hieros Gammos. ➤ **See p. 66.**

Jacques de Molay. Last of the Grand Masters of the Knights Templars. A non fictional character, but much of his life remains a mystery. ➤ **See index.**

Jesse Tree. A pictorial representation of the genealogical tree of Christ. Often seen in stained glass. In Paris see Notre Dame, Sainte-Chapelle and St Denis Basilica, see also the Cathedral of Chartres. There is a carved Jesse Tree in Cluny. The imagery is based on the prophecy of Isaiah (11: 1-3) that a Messiah would spring from the family of Jesse, father of David. Jesse is usually shown reclining with a tree growing from his loins.

Knights Templar. For the story of the Templars ➤ **See p. 114.**

Masons. The Masons are a society that claim ancient origins, certainly going back to medieval Masonry corporations. A document by the Archbishop of Canterbury

mentions the existence of freemasons in 1396. The Lodges in which they meet were originally the temporary shacks on the cathedral building sites. They employ a system of complex codes, symbols, rituals and rites that can only be understood by the initiated. They say they are not a secret society, but that they do have secrets. To join you must be male, over 21, have belief in a supreme being and have no criminal record.

➤ **There are Free Masonry museums in many cities, in Paris: Grand Orient de France, 16, rue Cadet, 75009, metro Cadet or Grands-Boulevards. Open Tuesday–Saturday 2pm-6pm.**

Meridian. Means midday. At any location, the arc on the earth at right angles to the equator passing from North to South Poles. All celestial objects reach their highest point in the sky here, the sun is on the meridian at local noon. To create your own local meridian choose the spot you wish the meridian to pass through, stick a pole in the spot, verify its verticality. Trace a perfect circle around the pole. The circumference will be that of the length of the shadow cast by the pole at a chosen time, say 10am. Mark the spot with an A. Watch the shadow during the course of the day and mark the circle exactly at the moment when the shadow falls on the opposite side. Mark point B. Join the points A+B with a line, divide the line in half. Mark point C. The meridian is the line running from the foot of your pole through point C. You can now build your own gnomon.

Merovingians. This ancient dynasty of Frankish kings died out in 751. The last Merovingian was Theoderic IV, and his son Childeric III was deposed. In France, these kings are known as the "rois fainéants" or the Do-Little Kings! *The Da Vinci Code* story is based on the claim that this dynasty was descended from the union of Christ and Mary Magdalene.

Mire du Nord/Sud. North and south markers of the Paris Meridian. ➤ **See p. 109 and 128.**

Opus Dei. Little publicised group till the advent of *The Da Vinci Code*, which was founded by a Spaniard, Josemaria Escriva de Balaguer, in 1928. Pope John Paul II gave independence and status to the church by making them a personal prelature in 1982. A personal prelature is a jurisdictional entity within the Church's own hierarchical structure. The pope also beatified Escriva in 2002. There are apparently some 80,000 members world wide. The organisation has been criticised for its recruitment techniques, often aiming at the young and the emotionally fragile. Numerary members who generally live-in, vow celibacy, practise corporal mortification with cilice and discipline (this is Silas) and have every aspect of their lives controlled, for example, contact with family is discouraged. Most give a large part, if not all of their salary, to the organization. Dan Brown includes the Opus Dei Watch Dog Website in his book, *www.odan.org*. This site makes gloomy but fascinating reading.

Phi. ➤ **See p. 139.**

Philosopher's Stone. Is metaphorical in alchemy, like the sword in the stone, it probably symbolises "that which contains unobtainable knowledge." The stone also refers to the raw materials that make the elixir which allows for the transformation of base metals into gold. A carved fountain at the Museum of Arts and Metiers shows a low relief ship symbolising alchemy, the stone is to the right of the mast.

Priory of Sion. ➤ **See St Sulpice p. 135 and Templars, see index** or to discover more about this intriguing secret society, join a Paris Walks Da Vinci Code Guided Tour. Saturday mornings 12 €. ☎ 01 48 09 21 40.

SmartCar™. Sophie drives a fashionable SmartCar, very handy for parking in Paris and quite a speedy get-away vehicle, although not much room for storing loot. The car was originally developed as a joint venture between Swatch and Mercedes-Benz in 1994. The prototype was to be electric but after difficulties, the petrol version was launched. The car is made by Daimler Chrysler at Smartville! Each one takes 8 hours to make, that is about 1 foot per hour. The standard French model is called the "fortwo" the model being launched

for America is an SUV and called the "formore", only to be purchased by those that own a "fortune"!

Tarot. Brown mentions Tarot and the pack's suit of pentacles. In France the most traditional pack is made by Grimaud and is the "Tarot de Marseilles". The cards are used for a game as well as fortune telling. There is no suit of pentacles in the traditional French pack which consists of coins, batons, cups and swords. Some versions, including the

Tetramorphe at Chartres

attractive arts and crafts "Rider Waite" pack do. Tarot is believed to date back to about 1450, the original imagery was Christian, but in the 17th century the pack was influenced by alchemy and astrology. The Marseilles Tarot dates from 1760. The card illustrated shows a goddess figure surrounded by the tetramorph, and is titled the world, perhaps as the feminine aspect of God.

Tetramorph. The four symbols of the Evangelists. They have their origins in the book of Revelations. A winged man is Matthew, a lion is Mark, an eagle is John and the ox is Luke. This symbolism can be seen on many churches, one of the most beautiful tetramorphs is at Chartres. In Paris one can be seen on the Pulpit of St Gervais-St Protais Church.

WICCA. A modern association of white witches. The witch: earth mother, nurturer and healer, was violently surpressed by the Church especially during the 16th and 17th centuries. Academics propose differing numbers of how many were executed or burnt. It is generally accepted that during some 12,000 trials, between 40 and 60 thousand were executed. Langdon says some 5 million, as he tells of Saunière's personal passion for WICCA.

The Codes

Anagrams. Probably used by the ancient Greeks, and by the medieval period were attributed with mystical power. Dan Brown's book is riddled with anagrams, they are supposed to reveal what is in a name: Wolfgang Amadeus Mozart = A Famous German Waltz God. Dan Brown says the Romans referred to Anagrams as Ars Magna, the "Great Art", this is just another clever anagram, of the word Anagram!

Atbash Cipher. Extremely ancient code. A simple substitution cipher where the 1st letter of the alphabet is replaced with the last, the 2nd with the 2nd to last, etc., till the alphabet is completely reversed, i.e. A is coded as Z, B coded as Y, C coded as X. The name Atbash is based upon the substitution itself. It is made up by pronouncing the 1st, last, 2nd, 2nd to last syllables of the Hebrew alphabet. This cipher is used in the Bible, in Jeremiah 25:26, Sheshach becomes Babel.

Hugh Schonfield applied this to Baphomet and found it made Sophia, see Baphomet above.

Baconian. In chapter 20 of *The Da Vinci Code* Langdon remembers his work on Baconian manuscripts. The 13th century English monk Roger Bacon wrote *Epistle on The Secret Works of Art and Nobility of Magic*. This is the first known European book to discuss cryptography. By the next century ciphers were in common use by alchemists and scientists as a means of concealing their findings. Bacon presented seven different methods for coding texts.

Caesar Cipher. Used by Caesar and by Dan Brown on the front cover of the first edition of his book. In the computer age this is an easy cipher to crack. The letters in the alphabet are shifted by a given number. This is similar to Atbash but there is no reversal just a shifting. If the given number is three, then C becomes A, D becomes B, E becomes C, etc. As E is the most common letter used, a message can be decrypted by working out the most common letter, equating it to E and then working out the given shift.

Da Vinci. Wrote many of his texts in mirror writing. This did not give high-security protection to his ideas, but at a time when many were illiterate it would have made it hard for anyone looking over his shoulder to see what he was writing. He was left-handed which would have made mirror writing practical in the days when ink took time to dry. It is far easier for left-handed than right-handed people to write in this fashion, although it takes practice.

Drosnin Michael. Wrote *The Bible Code*. Having made contact with the mathematician Dr. Eliyahu Rips, Drosnin exposed the theory that the Bible encoded predictions. He was so entirely convinced that there was a system of codes, he warned Yitzhak Rabin of the prediction of his assassination. Some months later the prediction proved to come true. The work has been derided by many, but despite this, some of the predictions have proved true.

Fibonacci Sequence. ➤ See p. 139.

Jefferson's Wheel Cipher. Around 1800, Thomas Jefferson invented his Wheel Cipher. This consists of rings containing the letters of the alphabet. Each ring can turn around a central axis. As long as your correspondent has the same set up, he can decode your messages.

Palindrome. A word that reads the same backwards as forwards e.g. wow, or mom, or a phrase such as "A Toyotas a Toyota"!, or "Cain a maniac", or, just perfect for *The Da Vinci Code* "Madam, in Eden I'm Adam".

The Templars' Code. The Knights Templars had a secret code that they used to protect their promissory notes and documents. It was based upon placing the letters of the alphabet around their emblem, the vermillion cross. This is very much like the modern "Pig Pen Code", an example of which you can see on the frontispiece of this book.

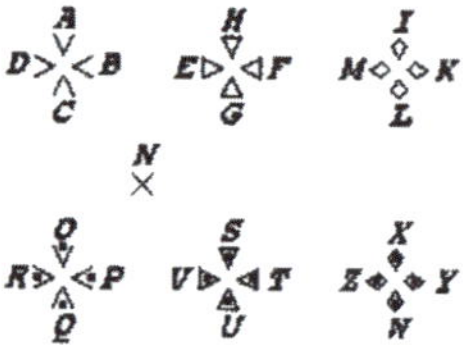

Vatican. The Vatican has used its own secret code for centuries. It remains secret!

Paris and its Grand Masters of the Priory of Sion

Between 1188 and 1963, 26 men are listed as having been Grand Masters of the Priory of Sion. Some of these have been particularly influential in Paris. Notably:

Nicolas Flamel, Grand Master 1398-1418. Well known for his involvement in alchemy, wealthy benefactor of Parisian institutions. Was buried at the church of St Jacques-de-la-Boucherie in Paris.

➤ See p. 107 and musée de Cluny.

Leonardo da Vinci, Grand Master 1510-1519. Not especially influential in Paris, but had huge influence on French King Francis I. It was to Francis that Leonardo bequeathed the *Mona Lisa*. Francis I was a kind and generous patron providing for the artist and asking only the pleasure of his conversation and ideas in return. Leonardo died in the beautiful Château of Clos-Lucé in Amboise. For a life of Leonardo see the Louvre section.

Connetable de Bourbon, Grand Master 1519-1527, enemy of Francis I, was put on trial in his absence and found guilty of *lèse-majesté*, rebellion and felony. His lands and possessions were confiscated. His arms were effaced, he was deprived of the name Bourbon and the door of his Paris town house was painted yellow, a symbol of his fall from grace. Bourbon won the respect of the imperial army who were in a mood of murderous mutiny having been unpaid for months. He promised to make them rich by sacking Rome. In fact, he attacked the pope in the Castle of Sant' Angelo. The mystery of just what he was looking for remains to be answered!

Victor Hugo, Grand Master 1844-1855. Much of his life was spent in Paris, but there were periods of exile during the reign of Napoleon III. In Paris, an avenue is named after him, and he lived there for a short while, his address being M. Victor Hugo, in this avenue, Paris!

➤ **For more on Hugo see Hugo Museum.**

Claude Debussy, Grand Master 1855-1918. Musician and composer who won the Rome Prize for Music aged 22. He is described as a brilliant but rebellious student. His early music lessons were taken with Mme Mauté de Fleurville, student of Chopin's and mother-in-law of Verlaine, who had much influence on his work. In the 1880's, Debussy frequented the symbolist poets and lived the bohemian life of an artist in Montmartre. The apartment where he was born can be visited, located above the Tourist Office (at one time his parents' shop).

➤ **In St Germain-en-Laye. See Debussy Museum.**

Jean Cocteau, Grand Master 1918-1963. Immensely influential in the world of the arts. Brilliant draughtsman, painter, poet and film-maker. Discretely influential everywhere. Cocteau was passionate about secrets and created a whole world of symbols in which he lived his life. He was very influenced by religion, surrealism, psychoanalysis and cubism, and loved ceremony and ritual. He became a member of many important organisations. In 1949, he became a chevalier of the Legion of Honour and in 1955, a member of the Académie francaise. At the Académie he had access to two librairies containing nearly two million ancient documents, manuscripts, alchemical works and some of the most creatively mysterious works of Da Vinci!

Isis and the Sacred Feminine

Cluny Museum

Mary and Christ by Pigalle (Saint-Sulpice) R.R.

SYMBOLS OF THE LOST SACRED FEMININE AND WHERE TO FIND HER IN PARIS

Carnavalet Museum

CARNAVALET MUSEUM *(History of Paris)*

23, rue de Sévigné, 75004, metro St Paul. Closed Mondays, 10am-6pm.

CLUNY MUSEUM *(Gallo-Roman and Medieval Paris)*

6, place Paul-Painlevé, 75005, metro Cluny-la-Sorbonne. Closed Tuesdays.

MUSEUM OF EROTICISME

(The author hasn't been there!)

72, bd de Clichy, 75018, metro Blanche. 10am-2pm.

SAINT-GERMAIN-EN-LAYE

(Prehistory to Merovingians)

Place du Château, 78100 Saint-Germain-en-Laye, RER St Germain-en-Laye. Closed Tuesdays.

LOUVRE MUSEUM

See also Isis in Louvre Section.

RESTAURANT

Our Gallic Ancestors (worshipers of Isis) is a lively restaurant on Ile St Louis, great fun for parties. Nos Ancêtres les Gaulois, rue St Louis-en-l'Île.

The following chapter explains some of the theory on which *The Da Vinci Code* is based. It examines some of the historical sources and indicates where appropriate examples can be seen in Paris.

Among the many fascinating but controversial themes explored by *The Da Vinci Code* is that of the "Sacred Feminine". This theme is the central core of the story, and two of its heros, Langdon and the Louvre curator, Saunière, are specialists in this field of study. We learn that Langdon has spent much of the previous year writing a book about the symbols and art associated with Goddess Worship. The title of his book is *Symbols of the Lost Sacred Feminine*. This is also the primary area of expertise of Saunière. We are told that he is "the premiere Goddess iconographer on earth" and that his contribution to the Louvre is "the largest collection of goddess art anywhere on earth." ➤ **The relevant collection in the Louvre is described in detail in the Louvre section entitled Under the Pyramids.**

When Sophie Neveu and Langdon arrive at Château Villette the first thing they notice is a statue of Isis on Teabing's mantelpiece. This ancient goddess symbolises his devotion to the subject. The importance of Isis and her relationship to Paris will shortly be explained.

Isis

The Sacred Feminine Eliminated by the Church

The Da Vinci Code is about rival groups and their quest for the Holy Grail. When Teabing explains the Grail as a concept to Sophie, he says that most people want to know where it is, but he argues that the most important question is, "What it is." He goes on to explain that the Grail is in fact the relics of the ultimate "Sacred Feminine", Mary Magdalene. Teabing has dedicated his life to the study of this and the evidence he uses as proof of his discovery is codes he sees encrypted by Da Vinci in his paintings.

Dead Sea Scrolls and Nag Hammadi Texts

These arguments are not a fabrication of Dan Brown's, but are based upon a long standing academic study. They are in part built upon the ancient Coptic codices found at Nag Hammadi in Egypt in 1945, and the Dead Sea Scrolls found at Qumran in the 1950s. Teabing argues that the significance of these texts is that they were written long before the council of Nicaea in 325 AD, when the texts to be included in the Bible were chosen. These rediscovered texts reveal things about Christ, such as his life and ministry that were well known but purposefully excluded from the Bible.

Transmogrifcation

Religious scholars argue that the rise of the Church was more than in part due to the need for political unification: one king and one god had to be a more stable system than that of countless pagan religions that divided people. As the Church developed, it adopted and then adapted important pagan rites and symbols, and slowly but surely these transmogrified into a new system of culture and belief. Langdon gives several examples: images of Isis with her miraculously concieved son Horus became the model for later representations of the Virgin Mary and Child, and the halos of saints were based upon the sun disks of Egyptian gods and goddesses. Evidence of this can be seen in the Louvre collections. The veneration of the Sacred Feminine seems to have travelled through the Middle East, the Indus Valley, the Mediterranean and then through Europe in general. There is a statue of Isis-Aphrodite in the Louvre. As the Church became the dominant force, Goddess worship was pushed underground. The Church subverted the role of its holiest women and Mary Magdalene was misrepresented as a prostitute. At Nicaea the Virgin Mary became the Theotokos or mother of God and was given a submissive role. The doctrine confirming her own birth by immaculate conception and her infant's virgin birth can be seen as distancing her from the pagan image of fertility goddesses and human intervention in procreation. God, Priest, King and Father would soon replace, Goddess, Queen, Priestess and Mother. "The Grail is the symbol of womanhood which has been lost, eliminated by the Church," says Langdon.

Goddess Worship in Prehistoric Times

There is plenty of evidence that Goddess worship is amongst man's most ancient activities. Statuettes and figurines representing the Sacred Feminine date back thousands of years. Some beautiful examples can be seen in the Carnavalet Museum in Paris. An exceptional figurine in pottery was recently found during the excavations of the prehis-

toric settlement at Bercy on the Eastern side of Paris. The Bercy figurine, dated at around 4,000 BC, is made of clay, and represents a female form with her hands resting on her belly. She is very obviously a representation of female fertility. Other examples of ancient female statuettes can be seen at the Museum of St Germain-en-Laye, just outside Paris. In the museum, they have a collection of stone figurines that are amongst the most ancient known, dating from about 23,000 BC. The collection includes one of the earliest and most beautiful representations to be carved with facial features, known as the Dame à la Capuche (The Hooded Woman), and comes from Brassempouy in the Landes region. It is dated to about 21,000 BC. The Romans also

The Hooded Women

Statuette 23000 BC

made figurines of mother goddesses, many of these are shown suckling a child on each breast. The figurines, mostly ceramic, were mass reproduced. Both the moulds for manufacturing, and the figurines themselves, can be seen in the above mentioned museums.

Fertility

For ancient man, reproduction and agriculture were the vital elements of his survival. The fertility of crops, animals and the human race were seen as divine and mysterious. The powerful act of procreation was also considered as mystical and therefore venerated. Procreation was miraculous and benificent, and it therefore could only be the work of God. The symbolism of these pagan rites was often simple and unambiguous such as the dancing in circles around the May Pole in spring. The culmination of this basic belief was a sexual rite symbolising a sacred marriage.

Prehistoric carvings from the vallée des Merveilles

Hieros Gamos

This rite was practiced by various ancient civilizations including the Sumerians, Greeks, Romans, and Celtic druids. A re-enactment of this was unwittingly witnessed by the young Sophie Neveu in her grandfather's house. At this point, she realises that he must be a member of a secret sect. The ceremony of Hieros Gammos is explained to Sophie by Teabing and Langdon as they escape to London in Teabing's private jet. When Sophie finally admits that she actually witnessed this strange and frightening event, Langdon explains that *Hieros Gammos* actually means "Sacred Marriage", a spiritual union through which male and female experience God. Langdon goes on to explain that the rite has been used for over 2000 years, since the ancient Egyptians initially venerated Isis. The unfortunate witnessing of this ceremony that revolts and frightens Sophie, leads her to cut all ties with her grandfather. This family rift is irreconcilable, despite Saunière's many attempts to contact Sophie.

Langdon makes it clear that what happened is evidence of the Priory of Sion's celebration of the Sacred Feminine. The idea of physical union as sacred has existed since ancient times. Examples of this can be seen in the Tantric rights of Hindu Yogis. There are also plenty of examples of the bridge between eroticism and spirituality in the decor of ancient Hindu Temples, for example the 13th century Sun Temple of Konarak, in the Bay of Bengal region of Orissa. Shakti is the divine sexual aspect of Kali Ma, the Dark Goddess of destruction and creation. The Lingam is a small altar or shrine that symbolises the vulva and the phallus united. The shop windows of the passage Brady, Paris' Indian quarter are full of these images and symbols. To visit Passage Brady and the Indian quarter, go to metro Château-d'Eau, or walk along the rue du Faubourg-St-Denis northwards from the gare du Nord.

Hermaphrodite to Adam

An example of Hieros Gamos exists in an ancient Sumerian Poem some 5000 years old. It describes the ceremony taking place between a priestess called "Innana" and King Dumuzi. The union of the priestess with the king in the temple celebrates the Goddess' acceptance of king as ruler of her people, and reinforces the divinity associated with the role of king. A Sophian Gnostic tract says that Adam is in a state of Hieros Gamos at the outset, being both male and female, like Hermaphrodite, until the creation of Eve. Dan Brown includes this ceremony to emphasise that it is the Church that gives the label "Original Sin" to what was previously seen as the divine mystery of procreation.

From Sacred Marriage to Christ's Marriage

Dan Brown's book makes it clear that Goddess worship and the notion of the Sacred Feminine have been inherent in man's psyche since his origins. The book goes further by emphasizing the following argument: the Sacred Feminine was so important that eventually Christ would trust the continuation of the Church to a woman, this being Mary Magdalene, to whom, according to this theory, Christ was married. The principal argument used by those that follow this belief is based upon the content of ancient texts among the Dead Sea Scrolls, and two particular extracts from the Nag Hammadi texts.

From the Gnostic Gospels "Gospel of Philip"

"The Companion of the Saviour is Mary Magdalene. But Christ loved her more than all the disciples, and used to kiss her often on her mouth. The rest of the disciples were offended, they said to him, 'Why do you love her more than all of us?', and further in the same Gospel the passage: 'And the companion of the Saviour is Mary Magdalene'."

In biblical times, kissing on the mouth was purpotedly the reserve of married couples alone. The original greek word "companion" meant consort or married partner. Grail scholars have of course made much of this.

Christ's Bloodline

The Da Vinci Code argues that the Church has been fighting ever since its origins to maintain its male domination, and has made every effort possible to cover up this ancient truth. It is argued that the very reason that these texts were hidden at Nag Hammadi is that they were already seen as heretical by the Church in the very early Christian era. This fact, Brown argues, has been understood by an élite of small groups or sects. These have struggled in the form of secret societies, using their codes, art work, and symbols to pass on the message of the importance of the Sacred Feminine. The Christian ideal of the Sacred Feminine is encapsulated in the notion of the Holy Grail. This consists of both the physical relics of Mary Magdalene and certain documents concerning her life and her role. Teabing tells us not only that Leonardo Da Vinci was one of the keepers of the secret, but that he headed a secret society, the Priory of Sion, whose purpose was to protect the secret and the descendants of Christ and Mary Magdalene. The secret is of course purported to be preserved for future generations in a complex series of cryptic clues in the artist's paintings. These clues are fully explained in the descriptions of his works. The descendants of Christ and Mary Magdalene, Dan Brown tells us, were the Merovingians: a powerful dynasty of Frankish kings who made Paris their capital.

Back to Isis

It is said that Paris owes its name to the Sacred Feminine Isis. For the Egyptians, the name of Isis meant throne or seat, and was therefore of special significance to the ruler. If there is truth in Dan Brown's tale, it would be fitting and logical that Isis was chosen to symbolise the capital of the Merovingians. Ancient texts show a temple dedicated to Isis in the St Germain-des-Prés area. A Gallo-Roman shrine to the Goddess is recorded at the foothill of Montmartre, named Lucotèce in ancient times. Isis also has figured on the coat of arms of the city, which can be seen today on a school building in the Marais, on rue Vieille-du-Temple. An ancient statue of Isis was kept in St Germain-des-Prés Church, and it is described in a book called *La Fleur des antiquités de Paris* (The Most Beautiful Parisian Antiquities) published in 1561. The Abbot of St Germain, Guillaume Briçonet, had the

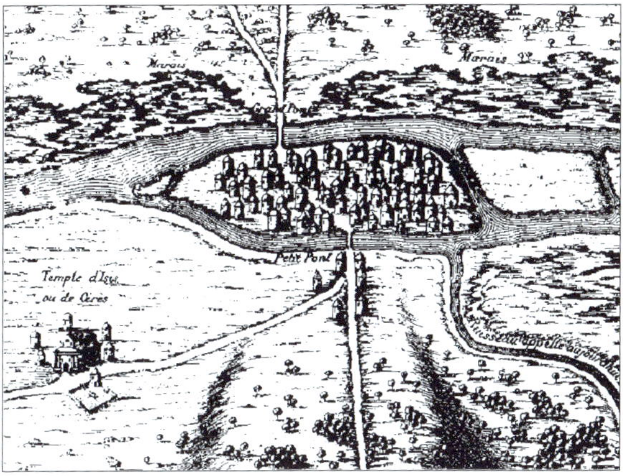

statue smashed in the 16th century. The lost Sacred Feminine of Paris was never to be replaced. By the time Isis had come to the Greeks, she had become the protectress of seamen, and recieved a rudder as her attribute.The founders of Paris, the Parisii were a powerful nautical guild who had a galleon as their emblem, and it is possibly because of this that Isis protectrix of seamen became the emblem of Paris. Carvings of the founders of Paris and their nautical guild can be seen on the magnificent Gallo-Roman pillar excavated from beneath the nave of Notre Dame. This is now kept in the Cluny Museum of Paris.

Isis, rue Vieille-du-Temple

The Paving Stones of Paris

Notre Dame

The Cathedral of Notre Dame

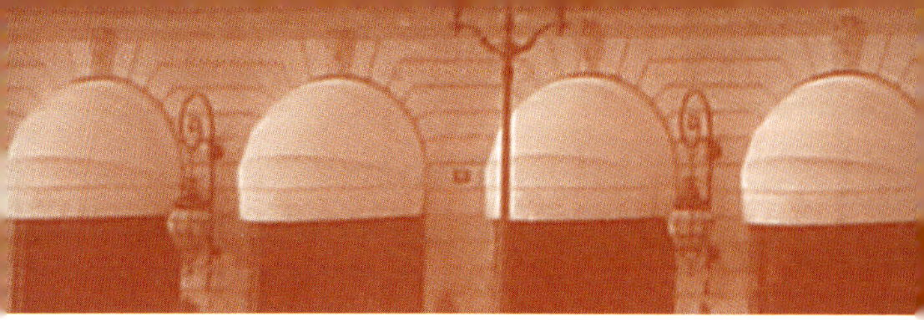

Sophie and Langdon in Paris
A Voyage of Initiation

Dan Brown has his hero and heroine travelling across Paris in an extraordinary manner. Critics have railed on about the impossibility of the journeys. Brown has Langdon leaving the Ritz and going by the Opera to get to the Louvre, which on a map appears completely impractical. He then has the police driving through the middle of the Tuileries Gardens which is of course impossible to do in real life. During the early part of the story, Sophie and Langdon make an extrordinary get-away from the Louvre. They dash off in Sophie's SmartCar™, they hire a taxi, steal a taxi and end up at Château Villette in a stolen armoured bank truck. Two choices are available: take the critics view and think "nonsense", or have a look at this journey in the light of Brown's book and see what it reveals! Drawing the route on a map, or following it on Paris buses, begins to reveal a few interesting clues: as they zig-zag their way across the city, they trace a series of triangles, both blades and chalices! At the Louvre, their circuit forms two pyramid shapes. They then circle their way along boulevard Malesherbes, rue de la Pépinière, rue d'Amsterdam, sail past Montmartre, and head along the avenue de Clichy to the exterior boulevards on their way to the bois de Boulogne. In doing this they trace a Fibonacci spiral!

Tour 1: Langdon Escorted by the Police: from the Ritz to the Louvre. The Itinerary

To retrace Langdon's steps start at 38 rue Cambon (metro Madeleine). The sites and monuments included on the trail are described individually below. This journey can be done combining walking and the use of city buses. From rue Cambon, head up to the boulevard de la Madeleine on foot, then follow along to place de l'Opéra (walk or bus 42 or 52). Take the beautiful rue de la Paix to get to place Vendôme, cross the square continuing in a straight line. When you come to rue de Rivoli, cross the road to enter the Tuileries Gardens. Continue straight on till you come to the central alley, turn left and keep going, walk through the Carrousel Arch, then turn to the side of the arch and take the entrance to the underground complex of the Louvre. Continue on past the ancient archaeological remains of the city wall (dating from 1380). In the distance, you'll see architect Pei's upside-down pyramid. Keep walking till you come up close, then, if you feel so inclined, like Langdon, drop to your knees with reverence (or fatigue!).

The Journey Step by Step

38, rue Cambon

This must be where Langdon began his journey, if he passed Opera to get to the Louvre. The staff entrance to the Ritz

Hotel is located here, a back door giving onto a quiet street. This is the security entrance that Lady Diana took to leave the hotel as she made her last fateful journey. The police have perhaps escorted Langdon through this exit for reasons of discretion; four star hotels do not appreciate policemen and suspects loitering in their lobbies.

Boulevard de la Madeleine

The boulevard is named after the Sacred Feminine! It takes its name from the huge temple-like church, The Madeleine, which is dedicated to Mary Magdalene. This was built by Napoleon as a pagan temple to the glory of his army. It is an imposing structure surrounded by a colonnade of 52 corinthian columns each measuring 20 metres. Napoleon later decided that the building should be consecrated as a Christian church, which was done on October 9th 1845, some 80 years after the building was started. Several iconic women of the 19th century lived on the boulevard. Number 15 was the home of Alphonsine Plessis, who was the inspiration for *La Dame aux Camélias* by Dumas and *La Traviata* by Verdi. At Number 32, Mme Récamier, Josephine's social rival, held her celebrated salon. Here Bonaparte's opponants gathered, including one of his own brothers.

Boulevard des Capucines

The name Capucines refers to a congregation of nuns once located nearby.

Further along at 35 bd des Capucines, the top floor of the building was the studio of Nadar, a pioneer of photography, whose beautiful portraits are amongst the most famous in the 19th century. Brown explains that the Impressionists painted in the Tuileries Gardens, and the first ever Impressionist exhibition in Paris took place in Nadar's studio in 1874. The paintings were ill received and the artists ridiculed. Nadar invented photography in artificial light, experimenting both in the sewers of Paris and the catacombs.

At number 14, a sign indicates that "the first ever moving pictures animated by a machine invented by the Lumière brothers" were shown here on December 28th 1895 (the name could have been invented by Dan Brown as lumière means light in French).

The Paris Opera: A Palace of Symbols

The Paris Opera is open to the public for visits. For a full guided tour contact Paris Walks. The building was commissioned by Napoleon III, but unfortunately for him, only inaugurated in 1875, after he had died in exile. He was never able to use the magnificent entrance designed so that he could take his carriage right into the building. This sumptuous palace is decorated with an abundance of symbols representing the theatre: lyres, masks with grimacing faces, and Apollo, god of the arts and creative energy. The building has always held a strange fascination, especially as it is built on a mysterious source of water which could not be drained away. This water became a lake which links to the sewers in Leroux's famous story *The Phantom of the Opera*.

➤ **The Sewers of Paris can be visited, see les Egouts, place de la Résistance, 75007, at the left bank, end of Alma Bridge. Closed Thursdays, Fridays, open 11am-4pm. The Opera, open every day except when closed for special functions, auditorium may be closed for rehearsals. Opening hours 10am-5pm.**

Rue de la Paix

The street was originaly named after Napoleon, but it was re-named after the Treaty of Paris signed in 1814. It is world famous for its jewellers, see Cartier at number 9. The fashion house of the Englishman Charles Worth was opened here at number 7 in 1858. Worth, who designed the crinolines of Empress Eugenie, wife of Napoleon III, was the first to show his designs on living models, the first one being his wife.

Place Vendôme

This is one of the five beautiful royal squares in Paris. It was built for Louis XIV, the Sun King. His symbol, the face of Apollo in the centre of a sunburst, can be seen on the iron

window balustrades. The square is typical of the classical architecture from this period: grand and majestic, with a great feeling for architectural harmony and proportions.

Langdon – Putting on the Ritz!

At number 15 is the Hotel Ritz, where Langdon is staying. Harvard dons obviously have very generous expense allowances or earn a great deal! The Ritz is one of the world's best and certainly most beautiful hotel buildings. Its façade was designed by Jules Hardouin-Mansart, whose family gave its name to the mansard roof. The hotel opened its doors to the public on June 1st 1898, and along with chef Auguste Escoffier, César Ritz soon created a palace of splendour and opulence that attracted a clientele of wealthy socialites. A peep in the guest book reveals: Coco Chanel, who lived here for 30 years, Hemingway after whom a cocktail bar is named, Scott Fitzgerald, Marcel Proust, Edward VII, Rudolph Valentino, Charlie Chaplin and Greta Garbo. The hotel was acquired by Mohamed Al-Fayed in 1979, his son Dodi was staying here with Lady Diana when she made her last fateful journey across Paris with him and their driver Henri Paul. Al-Fayed refurbished the hotel and created the new Ritz-Escoffier Cookery School.

Diamonds are a Girl's Best Friend

The square is famous for its jewellers. Opposite the Ritz, is Van Cleef and Arpels. The shops around the square have given inspiration to a host of Pink Panther style thieves and several generations of talented crime writers and film makers! Look out for: Boucheron, Chaumet, Guerlain, Schiaparelli, and Payot.

Medicine Magic and Mesmerism!

In 1778, Dr Mesmer opened his consulting room at 16 place Vendôme. A host of illustrious clients, including Marie Antoinette, came here for cures. The sessions began with his clients sitting in a ring around tubs of bubbling chemicals, they held hands in séance-like manner then pointed metalic rods in the tubs at an astrological map on the ceiling. The treatment offered was expensive, and Mesmer made a fortune. The success of the cures is doubtful though. History records the witty Parisian actress Sophie Arnould taking her sick poodle to see Mesmer. After three days the dog died. " Ah well," said the actress, "at least he died cured." Needless to say Mesmer was soon out of business.

Napoleon, Pillar of Strength

In the centre of the square stands the Vendôme Column. This was made for Napoleon from some 2,000 cannons captured by him at the battle of Austerlitz. It was a copy of Trajan's column in Rome, and Napoleon dreamed of having his own mausoleum in its base. The changes made to the statue on top of the column have been emblematic of the city's turbulent past. At first there stood an effigie of the emperor, but this was melted down to make the statue of Henry IV now on the Pont-Neuf. A *fleur de lys* was put in its place but soon changed for Napoleon more simply dressed in his military greatcoat. This statue displeased Napoleon III who replaced it with his uncle and predecessor dressed as an emperor once more. On the 16th of May, 1871 the members of the Commune pulled the column down. The National Assembly decided to reconstruct it in 1872, and they built the column that can be seen today.

Rue Castiglione and an eccentric Countess

The road is named after another Napoleonic battle, but was also lived on by the Countess of Castiglione, one time mistress to Napoleon III. The Imperial balls were her favourite pass time. She attended them in extravagant gowns, and guests would stand on chairs to admire her as she entered!

Langdon Spies the Eiffel Tower

The 1000 feet of the Iron Lady has the Harvard symbologist reflecting on the nature of the French. Langdon sees the tower as a phallic symbol! He says the French are renowned for small and insecure leaders, including Pepin the Short and Napoleon. Pepin is the king that bridges the gap between the Merovingian and Carolingian dynasties. The Eiffel Tower appears to have a quasi-mystical appeal, literally thousands of people climb the tower every year, and the authorities receive tons of mail asking bizzare questions. A look into the mail bag reveals a letter from a Turkish architect wanting to be told the mystical mathematical furmulae used for the tower's structure. The Washington Monument was previously the tallest building in the world, but the Eiffel Tower was nearly twice the height. When Gustave Eiffel died in 1923, it was still the tallest tower, and remained so for exactly 40 years. It was at last dethroned by the 1046 foot Chrysler Building in New York, followed two years later by the Empire State Building.

The Tuileries Gardens

As Dan Brown says, the name of the gardens refers to tiles that were manufactured here, made from the clay pits along the banks of the Seine. The area became a royal garden during the reign of Catherine de Medici. The gardens were redesigned in the 1660s by one of France's greatest gardeners, Le Nôtre. Walk along the central alley. Practical tip: Do not take your car into the gardens unless your name is Collet or you work for the French FBI. At the Louvre end of the gardens, there is a beautiful collection of sculptures by Aristide Maillol. He is the master of the "pagan sacred feminine" who eulogises the strength and beauty of women. Look for his fertility goddess *Pomona*, a nude figure holding an apple in each hand. At the age of 74 he met a 15 year old beauty who became his new source

of inspiration. This gave him a new lease on life! His muse, called Dina Vierny, inherited much of his work and has opened her art collection to the public. This is now the magnificent ➤ **Maillol Museum at 61 rue de Grenelle, 75007, metro Rue-du-Bac, 11am-6pm, closed Tuesdays.**

The Carrousel Arch

Dan Brown mentions orgiastic rituals here. The arch is certainly not known for this in Paris, but it may just be a personal experience of Brown's! The Carrousel takes its name from a special equestrian display held to celebrate the birth of the Grand Dauphin, Louis XIV's son. The arch itself was built to commemorate the battle of Austerlitz and was used as a ceremonial entrance into the central courtyard of the Tuileries Palace. As Langdon is raced around the Arch, he reflects on four of the greatest art museums in Paris. He says they can be seen from here: Orsay, Louvre and Jeu de Paume can be seen, but to see the Pompidou Centre, you need to walk a bit further. The bronze statues on top of the arch are copies of the horses from St Mark's Basilica in Venice, Napoleon stole them thinking they would look better in Paris, they have since been returned and replaced with copies. Stop a while beneath the arch and admire the truly spectacular vista from the Pyramid of the Louvre to the Arc de Triomphe.

At this point you can enter the Louvre taking the subterranean entrances on either side of the arch. You can continue your tour by following the guided tour in the

Louvre chapter. Before coming to the Louvre entrance, you arrive at the Carrousel underground shopping mall, where there is a large cafeteria, and plenty of catering options in the main Pyramid complex. The Tourist Office is located by the inverted pyramid, and toilets can be found in this area.

If you prefer to stay above ground, there is a pleasant café *Le Nemours*, under the arcades at the place Colette beside the Palais-Royal. Inexpensive lunches and good service are available, the café is next to the meridian marker of the rue St Honoré.

Tour 2:
Langdon and Sophie Escape from the Louvre. The Itinerary

Begin your tour by attempting to jump from the toilet window located in the Italian paintings gallery, between room 19 and 20 in the Denon Wing. Before escaping, Sophie looks out of the window and marvels at the sight of the Eiffel Tower, the Sacré-Cœur and the Arc de Triomphe, another mystical triangle in Paris. Admire the view before you jump, or if you prefer take the exit that Sophie and Langdon really use, follow signs to the Porte des Lions. This trail can be followed on foot and by city bus. Details of the sites and monuments are given in full after the itinerary.

Start at the Pyramid, walk through the passageway of the Richelieu Wing to rue de Rivoli. Cross the street and walk westwards beneath the lovely arcades to place de la Concorde, this takes about 20 minutes, or take a number 72 bus, three stops to Concorde. Stop at Concorde, walk to the central Obelisk for the marvellous views. Cross the square northwards to the corner of rue Royale and the square, to get to the Hotel Crillon. Continue along rue Gabriel, past the American Embassy, or take the 52 bus from in front of the Hotel Crillon, ride for two stops, get off and walk back along avenue Matignon to the Champs-Élysées. Continue to the Arc de Triomphe on foot or take bus 73 at the Matignon/Champs-Élysées intersection. Get off the bus at Étoile to visit the Arc de Triomphe.

Rue de Rivoli

The arcaded rue de Rivoli is named after a Napoleonic victory in Italy.

It was once lined with splendid shops selling luxury goods, but is now a jumble of perfumeries, clothes shops and souvenir boutiques. The road is one of the few new ones built during the reign of Napoleon. As Sophie and Langdon raced along the street, they had no time to stop, but on their return, they may have popped into elegant Angelina's tea-

room for an old fashioned hot chocolate, or one of their famous Montblanc cakes, which have become an institution in Paris. Angelina's is at 226 rue de Rivoli, 75001, between metro Concorde and Tuileries.

Place de la Concorde the largest square in Paris

Sophie and Langdon race around the square, having momentarily shaken off the police. In each corner of the square stands a colossal statue representing great towns in the different regions of France. The town of Strasbourg is a portrait of actress Juliette Drouet, long term muse and mistress of Grand Master Victor Hugo!

They pass the **Hotel Crillon**, one of the finest and most expensive in Paris. The guest book here is a Who's Who of presidents and royalty. The Crillon is one of two identical buildings on either side of rue Royale, to the right is the Naval Ministry. This was once the furniture store of the royal family. The building was sacked during the Revolution in 1792, and at this time the crown jewels were stolen. The square was host to the public wedding celebrations of Louis XVI and Marie Antoinette, it was also the location of the guillotine, first put here in 1792 to execute the thieves who had stolen the crown jewels. During the Revolution, 1119 people were beheaded here in two years. The eastern-most end of this building, bordering rue Royale, is the Hotel de Coislin. Here on February 6th 1778, a small group of French and Americans gathered to sign a treaty which marked the success of Franklin's attempts to enlist the help of France for achieving independence. The Treaty of Friendship, Commerce and Alliance made France the first nation to recognize American Independence. Strangely enough, the treaty was signed in the apartment of a man named Dean, who's Christian name was... Silas!

The **obelisk** in the centre of the square is some 3000 years old. The carved hieroglyphics make references to Ramses II, enabling it to be dated. Hieroglyphs were decoded for the first time by the French Egyptologist Champollion. It was brought here from the Temple of Luxor in Egypt, and erected in 1836. Transport of the obelisk and its erection (more phallic symbolism for Langdon to contemplate) were both incredible feats of engineering. The method of raising the obelisk is engraved in gold on the base of the plinth. The French astronomer Camille Flammarion planned to create a meridian here and turn the obelisk into the world's largest sun-dial. The first world war put an end to the project.

Sophie hopes to deliver Langdon to safety at the **American Embassy**, but seeing that the building is surrounded by police they turn back. The modern Embassy, in one of the most prestigious locations in Paris, was built between 1931 and 1933. The building originally on this site was the private town house of Grimod de La Reynière. This man was a celebrated "gastronome" who became the first official restaurant critic in history. It is he who advised restaurants that if you gave a dish a fancy name you could charge twice the price. On the 22nd of May 1927, Lindbergh made a speech from the Embassy balcony. Thousands of cheering Parisians had come to celebrate the first successful Atlantic Crossing; for more on Lindbergh see Le Bourget where Teabing keeps his private jet.

Champs-Élysées

As Langdon is driven up the Champs-Élysées, he "sat white knuckled in the passenger seat"; as any right minded person would, being driven in this part of town! The Champs-Élysées meant paradise to the Ancients. It became a huge open air theatre during Napoleon's reign, the road forming the stage, and the arch making the backdrop. It is famous for its shops and cafés, and is equally beautiful at night at which time it is referred to as "The Avenue of Rubies and Diamonds". Visit it at night to see why. The Champs-Élysées grew to extend the axis of Paris, which developed from the centre of the Louvre. It leads directly to another royal domain, St Germain-en-Laye, so called because it forms an ancient and mysterious Ley Line.

The Arc de Triomphe: a symbol of Paris

As Langdon and Sophie drive around the Arc de Triomphe the time is exactly 2.51am. 2.50 is a well-known clock setting to watch sellers. If a watch is set at ten to three, the hands form the shape of a smile, and the watch face looks friendly. This is a subliminal way to make the watch seem more attractive. But for Brown there is another meaning; not only does the shape make the form of the chalice he and Sophie are seeking, but as it is 2.51, the numbers add up to 8, the symbolic number of super-perfection. The watch is a Disney time piece featuring Mickey Mouse. Dan Brown mentions that Disney made much use of symbolism in his films, drawing parallels between "The Little Mermaid and

The Gallion, symbol of Paris (Musée Carnavalet)

Mary Magdalene". The initials of Mickey Mouse need no comment.

The arch was commissioned by Napoleon in 1806 as a symbol of the honour of the French Army. The architect who won the commision was Chalgrin, who was the man who finished St Sulpice. A recent guide-book to Paris describes the monument as Napoleon's magical temple consecrated to the gods of war. Grand Master Victor Hugo's catafalque was placed under the Arc de Triomphe for one night, whilst a circle of 40 poets stood in vigil. As the funeral cortège wended its way to the Pantheon, two million people crowded the streets waving banners inscribed with the name of his works. The flame of remembrance on the tomb of the unknown soldier was first lit here on the 11th of November 1923. At exactly 7.30 am, on the 7th of August 1919, Charles Godefroy flew his Nieuport biplane, with a wingspan of 8.22 metres through the 14 metre wide opening. This was a symbolic act drawing attention to the plight of pilots at the end of the war. Several famous pilots had considered the stunt including aviator Roland Garros, but balked at the attempt, believing it was too dangerous. To visit the arch, take the underpass located at the top right-hand of the Champs-Élysées. Climb to the top, the view is superb.

Avenue Wagram Boulevard Courcelles and Parc Monceau

From the Etoile, Sophie and Langdon race down to gare St Lazare. You can make the same journey by taking a number 30 bus. As you ride along the avenues and boulevards you will pass by magnificent Haussmannian facades, driving through one of the most elegant and expensive quarters of the city. This is also the diplomatic quarter where Sophie and Langdon career round the streets in their SmartCar before getting back to the Champs-Élysées. Rub shoulders with elegant society by taking the 30 bus from the corner of Etoile and avenue Wagram, and alight at Monceau. The parc Monceau, where the first parachute landing in history took place, is one of the most delightful parks in Paris, and it is full of curiosities. There are some of the most unusual trees in Paris: a plane tree with a circumference of 8 metres, an age-old ginko and a spectacular handkerchief tree. The gateway into the park is an old security look-out post from the Louis XVI city wall, which also houses useful toilet facilities.

There is a statue of best selling author... no not Dan Brown, but Maupaussant. Also, look out for the romantic ruined colonnade, part of the ancient Tuileries Palace destroyed during the Commune, which makes an attractive frame for the lake. There is a fascinating philosopher's garden thought to be designed in the 18th century by the imaginative gardener Carmontelle. This consists of iconography dear to Dan Brown: there is an obelisk, a pyramid and a tomb, just like the one in Poussin's painting *The Shepherds of Arcadia* and also at Rennes-le Château. Could this be the tomb of Mary Magdalene?

The area surrounding the park is full of sumptuous private mansions, many of which have become museums, embassies and consulates. One of the city's most delightful "off the beaten track" museums is beside the park. Musée Nissim de Camondo is a private collection of 18th century furnishings and objects that would be a perfect evocation of life in Château Villette. You can also visit the lovely old fashioned kitchens. The collections are laid out in a private town house left to the nation by a wealthy Jewish banker Moïse de Camondo in memory of his son who died in active service during World War I. His daughter and her family tragically perished at Auschwitz.

➤ **Nissim de Camondo Museum**
63, rue de Monceau, 75008, metro Villiers or Monceau.

To get to the next location get on the 94 bus from the corner of Parc Monceau and boulevard Malesherbes, and alight at gare St Lazare.

Gare St Lazare and Gare du Nord

At gare St Lazare, Sophie and Langdon manage to throw off the police, they buy train tickets to Lille, and then take a taxi from the side exit of the station. Trains for Lille leave from gare du Nord, and this is where Collet goes to wait for them. They are by now well on their way to the Zurich Bank!

As you enter the station via its grand façade, admire two modern art sculptures by Arman: a huge pillar of suitcases and a pillar of clocks "Time and Luggage – the nightmare of travel". Once in the station, buy a ticket for Lille using your credit card (preferably your partner's), tear the ticket into shreds, then leave the station by the exit marked rue de Rome, get in the taxi you have previously bribed and ask him to take you to Montmartre. If you prefer, take the metro line 12 from St Lazare to Pigalle. From Pigalle you can continue your tour by taking the Montmartrobus, which will give you a full tour of the village taking about an hour for the round trip. The bus goes by the picturesque vineyard, the Sacré-Cœur and also stops at the Museum of Montmartre. The bus brings you back to Pigalle station.

Sacré-Cœur and Montmartre

The huge Sacré-Cœur church dominates the hill top of Montmartre. Langdon and Sophie speed past it as they head on their way to Saunière's bank. This Catholic church was built by popular subscription at the end of the Franco-Prussian War, but not completed and consecrated until 1919. The biggest bell in the world, *la Savoyarde* is housed in the minaret-style bell tower. The architect Paul Abadie was inspired by restauration work he had been doing in the south of France on a Byzantine style basilica called St Front de Perigeux. The great dome can be visited (83m high), and after a long climb the look-out turret offers some of the most spectacular but vertiginous views available anywhere in Paris.

This area is one of the most attractive in Paris and is well worth taking the time to visit. In the 19th and early 20th century this quarter was home to Impressionists, Post-Impressionists and Modernists including Picasso, Van Gogh and Renoir. Picasso painted his masterpiece *Les Demoiselles d'Avignon* in his studio at the Bateau Lavoir in Montmartre.

N ROUGE
Féerie
LA REVUE DU MOULIN ROUGE

In *The Da Vinci Code*, the anagram of this work is "Vile Meaningless Doodles". Paris Walks offers regular guided walks here on Wednesdays and Sundays if you would like to explore the village in more detail.

Montmartre is one of the "hundred villages" that make up Paris and it has very much its own personality and character. There is a natural outcrop of gypsum rock here which was quarried till the 19th century. The quarries produced the famous plaster of Paris. The plaster works were located at the bottom of the hill, the area was always snowy white, and the square is still called "place Blanche" today. There is a metro here, a convenient point at which to start a visit of the village, it is also the location of the Moulin Rouge. The profession that Teabing says the Church foisted on Mary Magdalene, is also practiced here. The red light district stretches from Blanche to Pigalle. At night, the brash neon lights flash, the stores have runners on the pavement to entice you behind the curtained store entrances, and window displays show a variety of stange objects and some very impractical clothing (for over 18s only!). Watch your wallet in the red light district.

For a Sunday lunch and a glass of good wine in the company of a colourful local crowd:

La Mascotte 52, rue des Abbesses, 75018. On Sundays, retired builder "Florence" plays the accordian, keeping alive a wonderful local tradition. Good lunches available, service as eccentric as the clients! Florence is a medium and is probably the only person in the restaurant who can tell you if your food is actually going to arrive!

Tabac des Deux Moulins, 15, rue Lepic, 75018: this is Amélie's café in the film *Amélie of Montmartre*. The principal actress, Audrey Tautou, is tipped to play Sophie in the film of *The Da Vinci Code*. Montmartre always comes alive at aperitif time on Sundays, ie from about 10am onwards!

Off to the bois de Boulogne

Arriving at the Bois, Sophie and Langdon realise that the police are onto them, they are obliged to high-jack their driver's taxi. This is definitely the recommended way to get a cab in Paris, particularly at rush hour or on the many public transport strike days. The Bois is another of the beautiful parks of Paris. It is one of the "lungs" of the city, created by Alphand during Haussmann's reurbanisation project. Parisians come here for cycling, jogging and dog walking. Chic Parisians take the little ferry boat to have tea at the Châlet en l'Ile, on the island in the lake. As Dan Brown warns his readers, the park is best not visited at night, unless you know what you are letting yourself in for!

The Depository Bank of Zurich

They do have a website, but despite appearing conscientious about customer service, it seems very difficult to get through to them, and impossible to open an account.

Sophie and Langdon's guide to Occult Paris

Occult (c.f. Collins English Dictionary): of or characteristic of magical, mystical, or supernatural arts, phenomena or influences.

1. From the Island to the River Banks Some History

The left and right banks of Paris have very different personalities. The right bank is much larger (14 of Paris' 20 arrondissements, as opposed to 6 on the left Bank.) Paris was founded on the Ile de la Cité, where there is evidence of the Celtic Parisii having settled (➤ **See Carnavalet and Cluny Museums**). In Roman times, Paris spread to the left bank, the right bank being boggy marshes, beneath the flood plain of the Seine River. The left bank, a hill of high and dry grounds, was more easily accessible as the Seine is narrower and shallower between la Cité and the south bank. This meant that bridges could more easily be built. The Petit Pont near Notre Dame is the oldest crossing point in Paris.

The Roman city was divided into quarters by its two main streets, the cardo and decumanus. This is why the heart of the left bank is called the Latin Quarter today. A huge paving stone from the Roman road is embedded in the courtyard of the Church of St Julian the Poor.

In the medieval period, development shifted to the right bank. This became an important economic centre, boundaries of which continued to grow right up until the 19th century. By this period the flooding had subsided and the land had been reclaimed. The river, deep and wide between la Cité and the right bank was easily navigable, trading boats and ships could dock in this natural port. As goods were unloaded and traded on the river banks (la grève) this area became a huge and ever expanding market. The man in charge of trading and taxation was named the chief merchant of Paris, his sumptuous mansion was built on the edge of the market square, which developed into the building now called hôtel de ville.

Both the squares in front and behind this building were part of the market. When traders and marketeers were angry with conditions, they came here to "la grève" to manifest their displeasure, this is why the modern word for strike in French is "grève"! The money changers and bankers worked in the open air on the little square, place St Gervais, their symbol was the elm. It can be seen in the lovely iron-work balustrades along rue François-Miron, which runs beside the Church of St Gervais-St Protais, and an elm tree still grows in the middle of the square. In the 1180s the market was causing such congestion in the centre, that it was shifted further north, just inside the medieval city walls.

The market consisted of huge roofed barn-like halls, and is the "Les Halles" of Paris today. A huge feudal tower called the "Tower of John the Fearless", is evidence of the city's ancient rampart wall. The tower can be seen on the northern edge of the market today, and this wall formed the boundary of the right bank until the mid 14th century.

Paris kept growing and a ring of new walls was constructed around the right bank in the 1380s, (including the Marais), and again in the 17th century along what is now "les grands boulevards". The 18th century wall was Louis XVI's infamous ring of toll gates and the 19th century wall can still be traced around the city just within the modern day perimeter, which is the ring road now called the *périphérique*. For a "thumb nail" history of Paris, which is both beautiful and fascinating, visit the multimedia show ➤ **Paris-Story at 11 rue Scribe, 75009, nearest metro Opera. 10am-7pm, every hour on the hour, English commentary available**. You will discover Paris in the company of one of its most illustrious Priory of Sion Grand Masters, Victor Hugo.

2. Ile de la Cité

Itinerary

The Ile de la Cité is like a great ship afloat in the river. It is believed that the Gauls compared it to the boat used by Isis to seek her lost husband Osiris. Her story is told in the chapter on the Louvre. The following circuit shows the Gallo-Roman rampart walls, Notre Dame and its treasury, the Sainte-Chapelle, Point Zero and the site where the Grand Master of the Knights Templars was burnt at the stake.

Traces of the city's most ancient rampart wall can be seen in the archaeological crypt museum beneath the parvis of Notre Dame, and on the charming rue de la Colombe. This wall was probably built towards the end of the 2nd or beginning of the 3rd century AD, and was constructed from stone recuperated by the Romans from their own monuments. The remains of the wall are spectacular. A close look reveals some of the building techniques used: small holes and grooves were used for the insertion of lifting equipment and the fitting of huge metal staples to re-inforce its structure. Some of the most decorative stone blocks come from the old forum of Roman Paris. The wall was built around the Island to protect the city at the time of the Barbarian invasions. The main temple of the Roman city, dedicated to Jupiter, was on the eastern end of the island where Notre

Notre Dame

Dame stands today. Walk along the delightful rue de la Colombe to see a small mosaic of paving stones that crosses the street; this marks the location of the northern part of the wall.

Notre Dame, The Temple of Venus, Isis and the Goddess Reason

Notre Dame, built between 1163 and the 1220s is not without its own mysteries. The 20th century's most prominent alchemist "Fulcanelli" believed that the cathedral was a book in stone, "a Hermetic Masterpiece". He wrote that medieval alchemists used to meet in front of the right hand portal, and that the sculptures there are an encyclopedia of hermetic knowledge.

The cathedral is built according to a simple, pure and visually satisfying geometric plan. The architectural complexities of the golden section were known to the ancients and rediscovered in the classical period, but were unknown by the medieval cathedral builders. Masons building the church were sworn to secrecy by their masters.

Festival of Fools and other Pagan subjects

A group of strange sculptures can be seen to the right of the central portal. They allude to the annual festival of fools which took place here. This was a social safety valve to keep different levels of society in their place. Everyone got the chance to break the rules of convention. Sex, violence and drunkenness characterized the occasion; people cross-dressed, a pope of fools was elected, nobility dressed as the poor and vice versa. This sculpted group shows a female devil urinating on the heads of a king, a bishop and an ordinary man. The figures represent the three estates or principal classes, and the message is that even kings and bishops can go to hell if they do not behave themselves.

Alchemists and their Symbols

At the foot of the statue of Christ on the central pillar of the central portal is a strange allegory of alchemy. The figure in a circular medallion, is holding two books, one open, one closed. Rising from his lap is a ladder. The closed book symbolizes esoterism, the open exoterism. The ladder represents the hieroglyph of patience symbolizing the nine steps of patience the student of alchemy needs whilst working to achieve perfect knowledge.

Which hand?

The left and right side of the cathedral are associated with good and evil. In Latin, the word

for left is *sinister* and associated with evil. Spilt salt is thrown over the left hand shoulder so that it goes into the eye of the devil. On the central portal, all the virtuous can be seen on Christ's right hand side, and the damned entering the gates of hell on his left. To visit the cathedral, you enter through the evil side, on Christ's left, and leave purified through the good portal, on Christ's right.

Isis and Venus

Here Langdon and Teabing would be in their element! There is an astrological calendar in the rose window. It would be usual for it to begin with the sign of the ram, aries, but here it begins with pisces which is apparently a Hindu tradition. Pisces is the astrological sign of mysticism, and symbolises the union of the self with the universal soul; it is also the symbol of Venus in Greek mythology. The lunar cycle of Venus and Isis also appears in the Gallery of Kings beneath the rose window. The gallery consists of 28 kings, whereas according to the Bible, there should be 18 or 19. The lunar month of Venus has 28 days. Pisces also appears carved on the left portal.

Albigensians and Knights Templars

On the 12th of April 1229, Raymond VII, the Count of Toulouse, came here to swear before Saint Louis and Blanche de Castille that he would respect a treaty he had signed confirming his defeat, and his putting an end to the Albigensian Crusades. The Albigensians were Cathars, and as Brown tells us, believed that Christ and Mary Magdalene were married. The Albigensians were crushed during the early 13th century crusades against them. On the 18th of March 1314, Jacques de Molay, Grand Master of the Templars, and three other dignitaries were brought to the front of the cathedral before the king. The papal edict of the Templars' dissolution and confinement to perpetual imprisonment was read aloud. Molay began to proclaim his innocence saying that his confession had been extracted under torture. The crowd began to riot, and Philippe le Bel ordered him and 37 other Templars to be burnt at the stake. (➤ See p. 103)

A Pagan Temple

During the French Revolution the cathedral became a pagan temple dedicated to the goddess Reason! A five metre high mountain was built in the nave, upon which a model antique style temple was built. The temple symbolized philosophy, and its priestess was a dancer from the Opera called mademoiselle Aubry. She wore a white gown and a Phrygian cap. The cap, once worn by

The Synagogue

The Church

The Tree of Knowledge

The Funeral of the Virgin

freed Roman slaves, had become an important symbol of liberty. The cathedral was returned to the Catholics in 1801.

- **Notre Dame – The Towers, metro Cité, 9.30am-7.30pm. Open every day.**
- **Notre Dame Museum. (history of the cathedral), 10, rue du Cloître-Notre-Dame, 75004, metro Cité. Open Wednesdays, Saturdays and Sundays, 2.30pm-6pm.**
- **Crypte archéologique du parvis Notre-Dame, 1, place du Parvis, 75004, metro Cité.**

Point Zero

A brass stud located just in front of the façade of the cathedral marks the geographical centre of Paris. It is the point from which distances to outlying towns are measured. The plaque has become worn away as it is traditional to stand upon it and make a wish. Beware! your wish will definitely come true, the author stood on this stone 15 years ago, and has been married ever since.

The Sainte-Chapelle: Kings, Christ and Constantine

The Sainte-Chapelle is home to some of the best preserved stained glass windows to have survived from the medieval period. This spectacular building was constructed for the pious king, Louis IX, who had just negotiated the purchase of a collection of some of the most precious holy relics in Christendom. In 1239, the Crown of Thorns, part of the Holy Spear, and a fragment of the true Cross were brought to Paris by the king and his brother. The Sainte-Chapelle was conceived as a giant reliquary case in which the relics could be kept and displayed. It is impossible to date the building exactly, but there is evidence that the construction had begun by 1246, and that the church was consecrated by 1248. It is estimated to have taken about 6 years to build.

The chapel is built on two levels, the lower chapel was for staff and servants, the upper was the private chapel of the king where the relics were kept. The ciborium, on which the relics were displayed, can still be seen. It is modelled on the building itself, having its own lower and upper levels, the latter being where the relics were placed. They are now kept in the treasury of Notre Dame. There are twelve statues of the apostles, one on each of the main pillars, which symbolises that the apostles are the pillars of the church.

The Windows

The windows date from two different periods, the tall lancets around the nave are mid 13th century and the west rose is 15th century. The lancets mostly tell stories from the Old Testament. This is curious as the Old Testament on its own was seen as the book of the infidels! The stories are told from the bottom to the top of the window, and read from left to right at each level. One window telling a story not taken from the Bible is read from the bottom to the top, but zigzags from right to left and left to right. This is located first right as you enter the upper chapel. It tells the story of the relics, from their acquisition by Constantine in the 3rd century to their arrival at the Sainte-Chapelle in the 13th century. The rose window tells the story of the Apocalypse (➤ **For more information see the section on symbols**). The predominant colour in the glass is emerald green, which symbolises the throne of God as described in Revelation 4:3, where John sees God in a rainbow of emerald light. The throne and its accompanying symbols can be seen in the centre of the rose window.

➤ **Sainte-Chapelle, metro Cité. Open every day, with regular evening concerts. Concerts are performed in the upper chapel and this is a beautiful and atmospheric way to experience the building.**

The Aga Khan's Residence
Headquarters of a Mysterious Sect

The house standing here has some of the most glorious views in Paris. It is best seen from the western-most tip of the Ile St Louis. Although this building is made up from recuperated medieval architectural elements, it was built by a French architect called Ferdinand Pouillon in 1956. The architect lived here for a year before it was purchased by the Aga Khan. This is the title of the hereditary head of the

Ismailian sect of Muslims, who trace their origins to the tribe of the medieval Assassins. Ismailis are adherents of a secret Islamic sect, a branch of the Shiites also known as the Seveners which retains its own secret traditions and rites. Prince Aly Khan married Rita Hayworth in the Mosque of Paris. The Mosque of Paris is well worth visiting. It is built around a courtyard and garden and has a splendidly exotic tea room and garden. The minaret is 33 metres tall.

➤ **1-3, rue des Ursins, 75004, metro Cité.**

Square du Vert Galant. Kings and Templars

At the western end of the island, on the far side of Pont-Neuf, there is a small garden that offers spectacular views across the river and the west side of Paris. The square is named after Henry IV, whose nickname Vert Galant, is an allusion to his youthful verve and lust for life. The statue of the king was made in the early 19th century from the bronze recuperated from the statue of Napoleon that had stood on top of the Vendôme Column. The founder, Mesnel is said to have hidden the words of anti-royalist songs in the horse's belly and a statue of Napoleon inside the king's right arm.

The Curse of Jacques de Molay, Grand Master of the Templars

Steps behind the statue lead down to the garden, where the last act of the story of the Templars was played out. On March 18th 1314, Philippe le Bel condemned Jacques de Molay to death. Molay and three of his companions were brutally burnt at the stake here. The Grand Master called to the King, the Pope and his two ministers from his burning pyre. He demanded that they meet him before the court of God by the end of the year, and he went on to curse the kingdom and the dynasty. The terrible curse took effect. The Pope died in agony on April 20th, the king died after a curious hunting accident in November, the Minister Nogaret died in mysterious circumstances a few days later and the Minister Marigny was hung. Philippe le Bel's three sons died in quick succession, after short reigns, leaving only one male heir who died after a couple of weeks. Charles IV, last son of Philippe le Bel, died in 1328 at the age of 33, bringing an end to the direct dynasty of Capetian Kings and the start of a legendary tale of the power of the Knights Templars. (➤ **For a complete history of the Templars see under Square du Temple.**)

3. Sophie and Langdon's Right Bank

Bar Tabac des Templiers

The bar tabac des Templiers is a must for anyone with a taste for the unusual and a sense of curiosity about the mysterious knights. Teabing and Langdon would have felt at home here dicussing the Templars with the Grand Master of the Café, Jacques Serre. This slightly scruffy café museum has an incredible collection of jumbled objects, documents and paintings that evoke royal history and that of the Templars. Either side of the doorway, as you enter, are copies of the last will and testament of Louis XVI, there are documents about the trial of Marie Antoinette, and Joan of Arc is an important symbol. The Templars evidently discovered the Turkish style toilette on the crusades, and brought it back here with them! Here you can purchase a T-shirt emblazened with the Templars'crest, you can stand at the bar, sit down or go to the counter to place your bets on the horse races. The café is guaranteed to be filled with an eccentric crowd and occasionally the author of this guide. If you wish to get involved in a discussion on the French monarchs, be warned, there are both legitimists and Orleanists in France. The café supports the legitimists who hope to see a Bourbon on the throne. The Orleanists support the descendants of the last king of France, Louis Philippe. Open every day 6am-2am. ➤ **Bar tabac des Templiers, 35 rue de Rivoli, 75004, metro Hôtel de Ville.**

Bang on time! A Canon in the Palais-Royal Garden

The original Paris Meridian runs through the gardens of Palais-Royal at 2° 20′ 14″ east of Greenwhich and ahead of it by 9 minutes and 21 seconds. A small cannon was fixed on the meridian line in 1786. A magnifying lense in line with the sun ignited the powder firing the cannon at exactly midday, enabling Parisians to set their watches. In recent years, the cannon was fired by hand as the lense had gone missing. Part of the mechanism was stolen in 1999 and all that remains today is its plinth and the barrel. (➤ **See Meridian in glossary.**)

➤ **Metro Palais-Royal-Musée-du-Louvre, in the garden area.**

Catherine de Medici's Astrological Column and a Self-fulfulling Prophecy

The strange tower, topped with a cage-like astrolabe is all that is left of a royal palace once known as l'Hotel de la Reine, built for Catherine de Medici, who was a great believer in astrology. The untimely death of her husband Henry II had been predicted by Pope Paul III's astrologer Luc Gauric whose prediction was confirmed in a verse by Nostradamus. The queen appointed Nostradamus, doctor-astrologer, to her court in 1556. The two astrologers' predictions came true when Henry II died in a jousting accident in 1559. This re-inforced her belief in the occult art. The strength of such beliefs is illustrated in the word disaster, it comes from "Des Astres" meaning from the stars, and shows how the position of the planets was thought to affect daily life. The court organised dances and parades in special formation according to star charts. When Nostradamus left the court she employed Cosimo Ruggieri as her astrological advisor and had this 31 metre tower built for him in the 1570s. Ruggieri in turn would foretell the death of the queen. He informed her that she would die near St Germain. In Paris, the church of the Louvre was St Germain l'Auxerrois, and her country residence was St Germain-en-Laye, so she retreated to her château at Blois. Frail and worried

after the long journey, she took to her bed and called the new abbot at the château to hear her confession. When she asked him his name he replied, "Julien de Saint-Germain." She promptly dropped dead!

➤ **The Tower, Bourse du commerce, rue de Viarmes, 75001, metro Louvre-Rivoli.**

If you wish to know what lies in store for you or a friend go to **Astroflash**, at 84 avenue des Champs-Élysées, metro Franklin D.-Roosevelt. For a very reasonable price, you can purchase an attractive and surprisingly revealing astrological chart, complete with analysis. Open 7 days a week.

The Chapelle Expiatoire

The chapel is a tranquil harbour of peace tucked away behind the noise and bustle of the St Lazare Station and the department store quarter. It was built for Louis XVI's brother, Louis XVIII, in memory of the martyred king and queen, and as its name suggests, is a public request for forgiveness after the attrocities commited during the Revolution. It is here that Louis XVI and Marie Antoinette were buried after being executed, but much mystery surrounds what happened to them after their deaths, just as it surrounds Dan Brown's question of the Merovingians.

Originally the site had been the cemetery of the Madeleine Church, but its proximity to the guillotine meant that it soon became the communal grave for over 1,000 people executed at this time. Amongst those whose bodies were unceremoniously thrown here were Charlotte Corday, who assasinated Marat, Madame Roland, Philippe Égalité, Camille Desmoulins, and Danton.

Louis XVIII supposedly had the remains of his brother and sister-in-law disinterred and transported to the royal burial-ground of St Denis in 1815 some 23 years after their execution. The number of those buried here in addition to the passage of time would have made the bodies of the king and queen impossible to identify accurately. The other remains from the site were transported to the catacombs before the chapelle was built in 1816, and it is very probable that their true remains lie there along with 6 million other Parisians.

Over 100 people were killed in a terrible accident during the wedding celebration of Marie Antoinette and Louis XVI, which was held on the Concorde Square. These unfortunates were buried here in the cemetery and it is strangely ironic that those victims should have remained side by side with the king and queen for over 20 years. One thing is certain; this association of the monarchs with the Madeleine gives another string to Dan Brown's bow.

- **Square Louis XVI. 29, rue Pasquier, 75008, metro St Augustin.**
- **The Catacombs, metro Denfert-Rochereau, closed Mondays, (skeleton staff only) dogs not allowed!**

The locations of the Guillotine, the Patriotic Shortener!

The guillotine was moved many times during the revolutionary years, as it needed solid foundations and level ground in order to function correctly. Five paving stones can be seen in the street by 16 rue Croix-Faubin. The first guillotine was set up in front of the Hotel de Ville. For a while, it was located where the Carrousel Arch is now, then the Bastille and the place de la Nation. A real military guillotine can be seen in the café La Guillotine at the Caveau des Oubliettes, on rue Galande. There are guillotine blades in the Police Museum and the Conciergerie.

Nicolas Flamel's House Grand Master of Priory of Sion 1398-1418

Nicolas Flamel was Paris' most celebrated alchemist. One of his many properties, which is said to be the oldest house in Paris, is now a restaurant. Flamel was born in Pontoise, outside Paris in 1330. He was an educated man who bought and sold manuscripts and seems to have worked as a public scribe. He generated immense riches, and sudden wealth at this period was often ascribed to alchemy. In fact, the goal of the alchemist (turning base metals into gold) was not financial but spiritual. The hermetic and mysterious world of alchemy was one of symbolism and allegory. The transmutation of materials symbolised a spiritual passage between man's terrestrial existence and a spiritual one.

The quest of the alchemist was also related to a search for immortality. An immortality pill was initially sought using refined mercury sulphide. This resulted in many deaths! Alchemists encouraged the development of accurate scientific equipment such as scales, clocks, measures and temperature control, which were needed for their experiments. They thus contributed greatly to the world of medecine, chemistry and pharmacology. They improved knowledge of

dyeing, they probably invented fireworks and gunpowder, and discovered anesthesia and distillation. The English philosopher and alchemist Bacon is mentioned by Langdon to Sophie when they are trying to decrypt the messages left in the Louvre.

Flamel's career as an alchemist began after a dream, in which an angel brought him a book illustrated with strange designs, and told him, "You understand nothing in this work, no one else does, but one day you will see in it what no-one else can." Shortly after this, a stranger came into his shop and offered him a manuscript to buy. Immediately he recognised this as the one in his dream. It turned out to be an alchemist's almanach. Suddenly filled with desire to pursue this dream, he built a laboratory and began to experiment. He recorded success at transmutation, then made a pilgrimage to Spain and met Jewish Hermetic scholars. His great wealth, although mysterious, is evident because he became a generous benefactor, building porches onto churches, restoring the Cemetery of the Innocents in Paris, helping charitable foundations and opening an alms house, which is now a restaurant on rue de Montmerency. His tomb stone can be seen in the Cluny Museum. It was discovered at Les Halles when the market was demolished. It had been turned upside down and used as a chopping-board for shredding spinach. Flamel lived very near the tour St Jacques, the roads Flamel and Pernelle are named after him and his wife. The philosopher's stone, the secret of eternal life, is sought after by alchemists. Nicolas Flamel and the philosopher's stone are central to one of the *Harry Potter* stories, and recently critics have referred to *The Da Vinci Code* as the *Harry Potter* for grown-ups!

➤ **L'auberge Nicolas-Flamel, 51, rue de Montmorency, 75003, metro Rambuteau or Arts et Metiers. Closed Saturday afternoons and Sundays.**

The Mire du Nord

The mire du nord is the northern marker of the old Paris meridian. It is a masonry pyramid three metres tall. It was installed on the top of the hill of Montmartre by Cassini, the first astronomer to realise that there were spaces between the rings of Saturn.

It is difficult to access it as it is located in a private residence, although the guardian is supposed to let visitors in on request. The residence is at 1 avenue Junot in the garden of the old windmill where Renoir painted his famous work the *Moulin de la Galette*, now in the musée d'Orsay. Beware, an agressive concierge guards the access to the mire, take a clove of garlic in case!

The Picasso Museum

Saunière, though curator of the Louvre, was astonishingly no fan of modern art. He expresses his distate for cubism through the brilliant anagram of Picasso's *Les Demoiselles d'Avignon* which becomes "Vile Meaningless Doodles". Picasso would have been amused as the Surrealists and Dadaists all loved word play and this was evident in their art. One of Picasso's closest friends was Jean Cocteau, Grand Master of the Priory of Sion. Cocteau took the idea of being a member of an elite group very seriously, whereas Picasso did not. Picasso proposed a design for Cocteau's sword when he was elected a member of the French Academy. It was in the form of a toilet seat!

Picasso was the first to glue and stick real objects onto his paintings, including words and phrases cut from newspapers and magazines. This made him the inventor of another new art form dear to modern artists: collage. His first work in this style, called *Chaise canée* is at the Picasso Museum. The museum has a fantastic collection of the artist's work covering the whole of his life. Works range from his childhood right up to his final period. Picasso died in 1973 aged

92, and had worked prolifically all his life. The museum has purchased no works but is made up of a large part of the artist's private collection, bequeathed according to a French law called a "dation". This means his heirs gave the works in lieu of death duties. Picasso never lived here and had no association with the building, but owned several historic houses and châteaux and would undoubtedly have approved. The museum is laid out chronologically enabling the visitor to follow each of the artist's brilliant periods. Key works of the museum include: two **self-portraits**, ***La Fillette aux pieds Nus***, painted in 1895 when the artist was just 14 years old, ***The Death of Casagemus***, portrait of a friend of his who died shortly after Picasso's arrival in Paris. There is an entire room devoted to the development of **Cubism**. There is also an elegant realist portrait of his wife **Olga**, which shows he could do it when he tried! **Sculptures** and later works are displayed in the basement of the building, a beautiful 17th century mansion. The building is known as The Hotel Salé or Salty House, because its original owner made his fortune from administering the salt tax for Louis XIV.

➤ **Picasso Museum, Hotel Salé, 5, rue de Thorigny, 75003, metro St Paul. Open 9.30am-6pm. Closed Tuesdays.**

The Pompidou Centre

Langdon, perhaps keen on modern art, mentions the Pompidou Centre several times. As a symbologist, he would be keen to see the works of the Symbolists, the Surrealists and Dadaists for whom the world of symbols was extremely important. He would have also studied Paul Klee and Kandinsky, who invented their own symbolic pictorial languages, and be able to discourse lengthily on the suprematist Malevitch, who painted a white square on a white background.

The museum also has a collection of works by Yves Klein, who painted the first monochromes in his famous flourescent blue. There are a few beautiful Jackson Pollock dripping paintings too. Langdon would probably spend time contemplating the dark and strangely moving religious paintings of Rouault.

The Pompidou Centre is itself a coded building! The architects, Richard Rogers and Renzo Piano, used the colour codes of architectural plans to illustrate the purpose of each part of the building. Red indicates the moving parts such as escalators and lifts, green all the parts that carry water, yellow is used for all the electrics and blue for air ducts and conditioning.

The building takes its inspiration from Notre Dame and nearby St Merry. Like these gothic churches, all the structural elements are on the exterior of the building, leaving a vast open space inside for the museum displays.

The modern art museum was one of President Pompidou's projects. He was very interested in modern art. A competition was held to find the best design. 681 architects entered the contest. Only 20 were French.

Pompidou commissioned some ultra modern interior décor for the Elysée Palace, causing outrage amongst the traditionalists. A magnificent room designed for him by Agam is now recreated here at the museum, see the "salle Agam" on the 4th floor.

The museum is divided into two levels. The 4th floor shows art from the 1960s to the present day, the 5th floor displays work from the beginning of Modern Art (Matisse and Picasso) to the 1960s.

➤ **Pompidou Centre, 75004, nearest metro Hôtel-de-Ville. Open 11am-9pm. Closed Tuesdays. Spectacular views available from roof-top terrace.**

A Rosicrucian Temple

The Rosicrucians are another of the many religious sects that are mentioned frequently by Dan Brown. This esoteric movement spread across Europe in the early 17th century.

Two pamphlets printed in Germany around 1615 are attributed to a Christian Rosenkreutz (1378-1484). He claimed to possess occult powers based on scientific and alchemistic knowledge. He founded the order of the Rosy Cross and the pamphlet was used to recrute learned men.

The Rosicrucian Fraternity has existed in America since at least 1774. According to their own historical publications, they were led by a Great Council of Three. These included Benjamin Franklin, Thomas Paine and later La Fayette.

Benjamin Franklin was a member of the Paris Rosicrucian Lodge "Humanidad". Thomas Paine lived at 10 rue de l'Odeon while he was in Paris. There is a plaque there that reads: "Thomas Paine, English by birth, French by decree and American by adoption."

The Rosicrucians bring together, into one organization, the various associations of individuals known as hermetists, gnostics, pythagoreans, magi, platonists, and alchemists. They study philosophy and offer classes in astrology, the objective being to reconcile the mystical, the scientific, and the spiritual. They use a host of symbols including the blade and chalice triangles Δ∇.

➤ Their Paris bookshop and temple are located at 199 rue St Martin, around the corner from Nicolas Flamel's House and the Pompidou Centre. (Books, cards, incense, tarot cards, pendulums, crystals, music, etc.)

St Germain l'Auxerrois

There was originally a Merovingian church on this site dedicated to St Germain, Bishop of Auxerre in the late 5th century.

The present gothic church is an almanach of *Da Vinci Code* style sculptures, carvings and religious iconography. Outside the church on the north side is an extremely rare "Ball of Rats" ("Boule aux rats"). Only three are known in

France. The sculpture shows rats gnoring away at a ball that may symbolise the bread of life or the world in general. The rats are being surveyed by a cat in hunting position.

The church is also home to a wonderful medieval bestiary of creatures. Look out for dancing bears, fantastical birds, griffons, monkeys, wolves and dogs. At the rear end of the church, at the base of the roof, is a frieze with a sliced fish. This curious work alludes to the name of local benefactors, the Troncon family, whose name means "slice" in French.

In the porch is a statue of St Mary the Egyptian. Her story is told in Jacques de Voragine's book *The Golden Legend*. This work, a medieval encyclopedia of the lives of the saints, is alluded to by Teabing.

The curious and beautiful statue shows Mary holding a stack of loaves. She was a prostitute who sold herself to earn money to go on a pilgrimage to the Holy Lands. On her arrival at the Temple she was pushed away by an invisible hand, and told to go over the river Jordan into the desert. She stayed in the desert as a hermit and although she could not read, she was divinely instructed in the Christian faith. She lived for many years on the bread she had taken with her. Her clothes had long been in tatters but her hair grew and covered her nudity. After several decades in the desert, she met a monk called Zosimus, who gave her his cloak and promised to return to give her communion. When he returned, he found her dead, but a friendly lion appeared and helped Zosimus dig her a grave. This story is painted by Chasseriau in the lovely church of St Merry. ➤ **See p. 114.**

Once the royal family moved to the Louvre, this church became the parish church of the palace. The royal pew can be seen inside the church in the northern side aisle. Artists employed by the king at the Louvre were traditionally buried here; about 20 of France's most famous painters, sculptors and architects were laid to rest here, amongst them Boucher and Chardin.

➤ **Nearest metro Louvre-Rivoli.**

St Merry

Langdon and Teabing would have had great interest in this beautiful and mysterious church which is associated with two female saints whose stories may have come from that of Mary Magdalene. There is also an extraordinary head of Baphomet crowning the central portal of the façade, which itself is a riot of creatures: beatles, frogs, snails and lizards that crawl up the doorway. Teabing mentions the symbolism of medieval church portals saying they were seen as equivalents to a certain part of the female anatomy! When inspector Collet reads Teabing's notes he wittily remarks that it makes him feel like going back to church again! Baphomet is one of the mysterious symbols associated with the Knights Templars. His symbolism is explained in the glossary. This church has the oldest bell in Paris (1331) called "the Merry", which is located in a small octogonal tower by the façade. The church has a beautiful organ and French composer Saint-Saëns, who wrote the famous *Danse macabre*, was organist here for a while. Along the outside of the church on rue Cloître-St-Merry there are fascinating gargoyles. The corner of the church was notorious for its filth, squalour and prostitutes in medieval times. In *Les Misérables*, Victor Hugo has his young hero Gavroche die on the corner that this street makes with the church. Inside the church is a 16th century stained-glass window telling the story of St Agnes, patron saint of prostitutes. (The first windows in the upper row of the nave.) Agnes was forced, into prostitution by the Roman Emperor to punish her for her Christianity. Later when his son was ill, he called upon her to pray for him. This she did and the boy was cured. She can be seen in the window, shown like Mary the Egyptian, naked but clothed by her long hair. On the walls of the third chapel of the left hand side aisle are frescoes telling the story of Mary the Egyptian. Her story is told in detail under St Germain l'Auxerrois (p. 113).

➤ **Nearest metro Hôtel-de-Ville.**

Square du Temple and the History of the Templars

The square du Temple is a key site in Paris. It was here that the headquarters of the Paris Templars was located. The ancient and spectacular Temple buildings survived until after the Revolution, but tragically they were destroyed, probably because of their association with the royal family.

Rue Monsieur-le-Prince

Both Louis XVI and his son Louis XVII were imprisoned here. Marie Antoinette was kept here until the execution of the king. A poignant recreation of their prison cell can be seen at the **Carnavalet Museum**. Today all that remains of the Paris Temple is a pleasant square, a covered market and a few medieval streets. The Templars compound was literally a city within the city. The limits of the enclosure followed the streets around the present square: rue du Temple, rue de Picardie, rue de Bretagne and rue Bérenger. The massive fortress and keep were located at the crossroads of the rue Eugène Spuller and the rue Perrée at the south-eastern corner of the lovely garden (square du Temple). The castle was built in the 1260s, which is later than both the Louvre and Notre Dame. Its size and stature reflected both the political strength and the financial assets of the order. The Conciergerie on Ile de la Cité gives an idea of what the Temple Building looked like. Its magnificent gothic chamber, called the salle des Gendarmes, and the huge feudal towers on its façade, were built for Philippe le Bel.

➤ **The Knights Templars Guardians of the Grail.**

The origin of the Templars goes back to 1118, when nine French knights decided to devote their lives to protecting pilgrims on their perilous journey to the Holy Lands. Pilgrims had been travelling there since the Christianisation of Europe. The city of Jerusalem, where Christ died and was resurrected, was the most important. A shrine had been built by Constantine around Christ's tomb; this and Golgotha attracted many pilgrims and accounts of their journeys exist from as early as the 4th century. Pilgrims carried staffs and wore cloaks with badges from the shrines they had visited. A collection of these badges can be seen in the **Cluny Museum**, many of them were found when the Seine was dredged. In 396 St Jerome, who translated the Bible into Latin, built two monasteries to accommodate the ever growing crowds.

In the 7th century the Muslim Empire grew to include Palestine, Syria and Egypt. Calife Omar took Jerusalem in 637, and during this expansion many churches were destroyed and Jerusalem became an important Muslim centre. The Holy Sepulchre was spared because the Coran recognises the sacred character of the teachings of Jesus. Pilgrimages continued through the reign of Charlemagne even though these were troubled times.

The situation for pilgrims changed dramatically when the Fatimids took Jerusalem in 969. The Calife Al-Hâkîm, known for his brutality, destroyed the Holy Sepulchre and persecuted both Jews and Christians. As news of the situation filtered back to the Christian West there was outrage. The Byzantine Empire, occupied with its own wars with the Muslim Turks, was unable to intervene in the Holy Lands. Christian Europe was obliged to take action.

The First Crusades

Pilgrimages had by now become impossible, and massacres were frequent. In 1095, Pope Urban II called upon Christians to conquer the Holy City once again. Neither king nor emperor replied, but feudal lords and dukes rallied to the call and prepared to depart. "God wills it," shouted the crowds. In August 1096, the journey began. It took three years for some 12,000 men to arrive. Jerusalem was recaptured on the 15th of July 1099. These men wore red crosses cut from cloth that were sewn onto their tunics. The name crusade comes from the French word "croix" meaning cross.

One of the leaders of these men, Godefroy de Bouillon, was elected head of the "kingdom of Jerusalem". According to some sources, he is also the founder of the Priory of Sion, and a Merovingian descendant of Christ and Mary Magdalene. He ordered the Knights Templars to retrieve the sangreal documents from beneath the Temple in order to provide the Merovingians with proof that they did indeed have a hereditary link with Jesus. Godefroy de Bouillon died shortly after the taking of the city and was succeeded by his brother Baudoin. Pilgrims once again came, now travelling by ship, but on land there were still dangers. This is why in 1118 Hugues de Payns formed an order of knights to protect Christian pilgrims. They named themselves the Poor Knights of Christ. Their fame spread and soon Baudoin II (cousin of Baudoin I) offered them room in his palace where Solomon's Temple once stood. Not long after this he left them the whole palace and they renamed themselves the Knights of the Temple. At last they had full access to the treasure they were seeking.

The knights saw themselves as both warriors and monks. In 1127, Hugues de Payns requested official recognition from the pope. The order had increased in numbers and organization became a necessity. The warrior monks would adopt a rule championed by St Bernard, and a hierarchical structure based on their social rank when they joined. A uniform was adopted consisting of a white tunic, with black or brown cloak, and their distinctive vermillion cross. In 1139, Pope Innocent II authorised the Templars to build their own oratories and have their own cemeteries. The chapels they built were simple, as was dictated by their adopted rule. The Temple churches were often round, as was the case in Paris, and is still the case in London. They were based on the architecture of Christ's Holy Sepulchre. As the order grew so did their wealth and independence. They played the role of bankers, and in Paris the Temple looked after the treasury of the king. Their political and religious independence would eventually lead to a decline in their popularity and disastrously, to their being distrusted by king and pope.

Other nations formed their own groups which lead to conflict, and the Hospitallers and the Teutonic knights warred with the Templars. In 1229, Frederic II Hohenstaufen usurped the throne of Jerusalem, having himself crowned at the Holy Sepulchre. He was supported by the Teutonic knights, but was excommunicated by the pope, and therefore hostilities ensued.

In 1244, Jerusalem was again attacked by the Turks. Jerusalem was lost again, and 312 Templars out of 348 lost their lives. Hope grew as the 7th crusade began, but this turned out to be a disaster, added to by the Nile flood which caused a terrible epidemic of dysentry. The army perished, king Saint Louis was taken prisoner, and the Grand Master of the Temple died.

In 1288, the Mamalouks launched an offensive against the Holy Lands, the Sultan Al-Ashraf took St Jean d'Acre in the spring of 1291 with an army of some 220, 000 men. Despite a reconciliation that united their force, the Hospitallers and the Templars fell. Guillaume de Beaujeu, the last Temple Grand Master to serve in the Holy Lands, was killed, as was the Master of the Hospitallers. The survivng Templars left the Holy Lands for the last time.

The Treasure of the Templars

From the end of the 12th century to the end of the 13th century, the Temple of Paris held the treasury of the king and acted as bankers. The Knights' own wealth, added to that of donations and gifts, made them an immensely wealthy and powerful organisation. Payments made to them by pilgrims for "safe conduct" was another considerable source of revenue.

But what was the treasure really? Some argue that it was the Holy Grail. The Grail consists of documents, including the famous Q document, said to be written in Christ's own hand, diaries of Mary Magdalene, and proof that Mary Magdalene and Christ engendered a bloodline of (sangreal) descendants.

Part of the Grail is said to be the sarcophagus containing Mary Magdalen's relics. It may also have included the arc of the covenant. All these were purportedly found by the Templars when they had the Temple as their headquarters. The tomb in the Poussin painting *Et In Arcadia Ego* and an actual tomb just like it at Rennes-le-Château suggested to the authors of *The Holy Blood and The Holy Grail* that the treasure may have been hidden at Rennes-le-Château and found by Bérenger Saunière.

Philippe le Bel and the fall of the Templars. Friday the 13th. (Philip the Fair, 1285-1314)

As a result of war, and a desire to extend his boundaries, Philippe le Bel was always desperately in need of money. He had obliged his financiers (the Templars) to collect taxes for him, which had in part contributed to their decline in popularity. Philippe fell into conflict with Pope Boniface VIII over clerical taxes and was excommunicated in 1303.

After the death of Pope Benedict XI, a French man, Clément V from Bordeaux became pope and settled at Avignon. Owing his election to the king, the pope agreed upon the dissolution of the Templars. Philippe IV had already persecuted the Jews and Lombardy bankers to obtain their fortunes, he now determined to acquire the great wealth of the Templars. Philippe argued that as they had lost the Holy Lands, their wealth no longer served any purpose. In a hugely successful secret operation, all French Templars were arrested at dawn on Friday the 13th 1307. Since this event, a superstitious belief has been attatched to that particular date.

Tremendous coordination was essential, and the arrests were planned long in advance. Some argue that this was not only done for financial gain, but in order to suppress the controversial knowledge that the Templars held. As each Grand Master was arrested, the king installed one of his own

administrators in each headquarters. In Paris, the chancellor Nogaret personally arrested Jacques de Molay. Templars from about 3000 different locations were arrested on the same day, and at the same time, in a brilliantly orchestrated seizure.

The arrest of the Templars in 1307 did not bring an end to the story. There were trials, tortures, and confessions. Parisians were informed of the evil deads purpetuated by the Templars. They were accused of blasphemy, obscene rites, and worshiping an idol named Baphomet. Spitting on the cross and sodomy were also amongst the crimes supposedly committed. 138 Paris Templars were interrogated in the lower chamber of the Parisian Templars' Headquarters, 36 prisoners died under torture and out of 138, only 3 denied the crimes of which they were accused. The evidence was conclusive: the Templars were guilty.

Several years of prevarication between king and pope would pass by whilst they squabbled over what would happen to the Templars' treasure. On the 22nd of December 1312, Clement V delegated his power to three cardinals, all of whom were close to Philippe le Bel. The fate of the Templars was sealed, but then again, so was the king's.

The last act of this incredible tale is told at the site where it takes place (➤ **See square du Vert Galant p. 103**).

The Church of St Gervais-St Protais. The Elm

St Gervais-St Protais is a lovely church situated just behind the Hotel de Ville. The two saints were Christian twins martyred by the Roman Emperor Nero. An elm tree grows in the middle of the square in front of the church, which was traditionally the emblem of bankers, but is also associated with the mystery of the Holy Grail.

The Priory of Sion are said to have disowned their protegés, the Templars, after the loss of Jerusalem in 1187. The Templars from this time onwards were no longer the military arm of the Priory, and no longer under its control. Which of the two parties held the treasure at this time is not known, but the Priory seems to have moved its headquarters to the medieval citadel of Gisors. At Gisors, a bizarre ceremony took place in 1188, which included the cutting down of a sacred elm tree said to be 800 years old. The felling of the tree is supposed to have symbolised the cutting of relations between the two groups. Until this time, Priory and Templars had the same Grand Master, but from this date onwards the connection ends. According to the Priory documents, the first Grand Master was Jean de Gisors and this newly formed Priory also went by the name of Ormus.

Orme means "elm" in French and Ormus is also an important symbol for Gnostics and Zoroastrians. According to the masons, Ormus is an ancient Alexandrian mystic.

There are elm trees in the ironwork of the building here and elms are also carved into the misericords (choir stall seats) inside.

Shrouded in Mystery!

The Turin Shroud has given rise to many of the theories developed in *The Da Vinci Code*. There is a full size reproduction of the shroud in the Church of St Gervais-St Protais. One theory says that the shroud was made by Leonardo Da Vinci and is in fact a self portrait.

The inexplicable crease line across the neck was supposedly put there to reinforce Da Vinci's unorthadox religious approach. The line alludes to the severed head of John the Baptist, a figure that in his paintings he gives more importance to than Christ.

Another theory is that the shroud was created when Jacques de Molay's body was wrapped after his crucifixion. The story is that Jacques de Molay was not in fact burnt at the stake, but mocked and crucified like Christ, then wrapped in a shroud that fused the chemicals found in human blood and in incense, to form the image of the man's body. As eccentric and questionable as these theories are, there is still no satisfactory explanation as to exactly how the shroud may have come about. The church bookshop, on the rue des Barres, has several documents about the shroud. They are all as evasive as each other when it comes to giving concrete information about this strange and ghostly object.

The Tour St Jacques

The tour St Jacques was once part of the church of the local corporation of butchers who were located at the nearby market. St Jacques-de-la-Boucherie Church was demolished at the end of the Revolution and the 50 metre high tower is all that remains. St Jacques was the patron of one of the

most important pilgrimage shrines in medieval Europe, and the tower was the assembly point for pilgrims as they prepared to depart for St Jacques de Compostella. The symbol of the pilgrims going to Compostella was the cockle shell, in French the "coquille St Jacques"!

The tower is supposed to hold secrets for alchemists. Nicolas Flamel (➤ **See index**) built a porch with strange figures carved on it. He was also buried at the church and his tombstone can be seen in the Cluny Museum. The tower attracts mediums and mystics of all kinds; perhaps they are the only ones that can penetrate the mystery of the building which is forever under scaffolding.

The tower has had a chequered history. Pascal carried out his barometric experiments here in 1648. He was a Jansenist, and like Silas in *The Da Vinci Code*, practised self mortification, dying after sufferings aggravated by this regime. There is a statue of him at the base of the tower. He also invented history's first ever calculator, which can be seen at the ➤ **Musée des Arts and Metiers.**

When Revolutionaries wanted to recuperate the bronze of the bells, they burnt the timbers so that the bells would fall, which they did, right through four floors of the gothic vaulting! The tower has been hollow ever since. It was then used as a bullet factory. A foundry was set up at the top and lead was dropped in small quantities into vats of water below so that the droplets would cool. In 1836, this architectural curio was bought by the city of Paris and proclaimed a historic monument. The architect Ballu began restoring it in the 1850s and the work continues!

The medieval tetramorph that once crowned the tour St Jacques is now in the gardens of the Cluny Museum. The tower is now a metereological station attached to the observatory of Montsouris.

Victor Hugo (Grand Master of the Priory of Sion 1844-1885)

Hugo occupied an apartment on the second floor of a lovely pavillion on the place des Vosges. This is now a museum and can be visited. Entrance is free. A long suite of rooms, one after the other, runs from an antechamber, through living rooms, to his bedroom. This room contains the bed in which he died. The rooms are dark and the atmosphere is oppressive and spooky. This is heightened by massive pieces of fantastic and imaginative furniture dreamed up by Hugo in an antique style. A mysterious and magnificent panelled room was made by Hugo for his mistress Juliette Drouet. The panels are in Chinese style and are filled with figures of acrobats and tumblers performing actions that make shadows, which form the initials of Hugo and Juliette. It is well known that Hugo took a great deal of interest in the spirit world, particularly after the tragic death of his beloved daughter Leopoldine. She and her husband drowned in a boating accident shortly after their marriage.

A friend of his, Delphine de Girardin, came to visit him and introduced him to spiritism and table turning. For two years he held regular séances, and was a firm believer that he was in contact with the spirit world. He spoke to his daughter but also Joan of Arc, Shakespeare, and Jean-Jacques Rousseau. The spirits dictated verse to him which was all in Hugolian style!

During a séance, a friend collapsed in a fit of madness and Mme Hugo soon put her foot down, bringing an end to Hugo's spirit adventure.

➤ **Musée Victor-Hugo, 6, place des Vosges, 75004, nearest metro St Paul.**

Place des Vosges

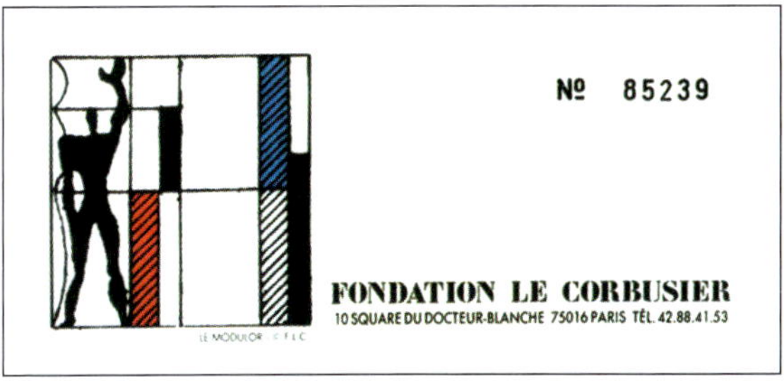

The Modulor designed by Le Corbusier

Le Corbusier Foundation. Architects and the Vitruvian Man

The Vitruvian Man is an essential part of *The Da Vinci Code*. He is the keystone that links together the series of codes that Saunière leaves behind, which send Sophie and Langdon to Da Vinci, the painter, but which also helps them decrypt his use of the Fibonacci sequence. Saunière's body is splayed like a pentacle directing them to the Sacred Feminine because the five pointed star is the symbol of Venus.

The drawing shows man against a framework that illustrates how nature has fitted its creations into the divine proportion of the golden mean. Langdon explains this in a lengthy lecture to his students. *The Vitruvian Man* was drawn about 1490 and is named after the Roman architect and theorist Vitruvius who served under Julius Caesar. His work was of little importance in his day, but was of enormous influence from the Renaissance onwards.

The Vitruvian Man is the emblem on the Italian one euro coin. Architects and artists driven by the search for perfection have all sought formulas to achieve this. In the 1950s, the architect Le Corbusier advanced a system of proportion that he called the Modulor. It too is based upon the human figure and was used to determine the proportions of building units. Le Corbusier's architecture, startlingly modern in its own day, can be seen all over France. Two stunning houses in Paris built by Le Corbusier are open to the public, where his design work, paintings and architectural conception are exhibited to their best effect.

➤ **Villa La Roche and Fondation Le Corbusier, 8, square du Docteur-Blanche, 75016, nearest metro Ranelagh or Jasmin.**

4. Sophie and Langdon's Left Bank

American University

The American University of Paris was founded in 1962, and is the oldest institution of its kind in Europe. Langdon has come here as one of its prestigious guest lecturers to talk on pagan symbolism at Chartres Cathedral. The University offers a complete art history curriculum.

Before Langdon speaks, he is given the kind of introduction that every lecturer dreads! Perhaps another personal experience of Brown's.

AUP is an urban institution consisting of a campus of six buildings near the Eiffel Tower and the river Seine. They offer a full complement of liberal arts subjects from anthropology to astronomy, though so far they do not include "symbology" in their catalogue. As they are an independent college of liberal arts and sciences, it is likely that the course will soon be available!

The Cluny Museum of Medieval Art

The Cluny is a must for anyone interested in medieval Paris. Many of the subjects covered by Brown are exhibited in the museum. Few objects of ordinary every day medieval life have survived, but the treasures belonging to the church were safely guarded. Here you can see relics and reliquary caskets, pilgrim badges, beautiful tapestries, altarpieces, medieval armour, as would have been used by the Templars, stained glass windows and much more.

The museum contains the tombstone of medieval alchemist Nicolas Flamel and the magnificent tapestry, *The Lady and the Unicorn*, subject of another best-seller by Tracy Chevalier. The building itself is medieval, and was built about the time Flamel was Grand Master of the Priory of Sion. By this time the Templars had long been disbanded. The man who built it, Jacques d'Amboise, had the cockle shell of St Jacques de Compostella as his emblem.

You can see this on the stairs of the courtyard of the building, where there is also a "wild man" well, and an early sundial.

The museum has good facilities, and an excellent book and gift shop.

➤ **Nearest metro Cluny-la-Sorbonne.**

The Cour du Commerce St André and the Guillotine

This charming labyrinth of little medieval streets is a marvelous relic of ancient Paris. Le Procope, the oldest café in Paris is situated here. Intellectuals and revolutionaries gathered here, many of whom were freemasons. Remains of the city's most ancient rampart wall can be seen in one of the boutiques in the form of a huge round tower. This wall was built by crusading King Philip Augustus in the 1180s. This was the time when the split took place between the Priory and the Templars and when Jean de Gisors became Priory Grand Master.

A plaque is visible showing where Guillotin invented and perfected the machine that would bring the monarchy in France to its tragic end. It is said that when the king was executed on Concorde Square in January 1793, an unknown man lept onto the scaffold, dipped his hands into the king's blood, and cried, "Jacques de Molay thou art avenged." A portrait of Guillotin can be seen in the **Carnavalet** Museum's revolutionary collection. He experimented for two years on lambs, which apparently have a similar neck to that of humans! The doctor was a humane man, a freemason, who sought to find a method of execution that was quick and clean, democratic, and far less barbaric than methods previously used. In the early days of the Revolution, his invention was given the seal of approval by Louis XVI himself!

The last public execution in Paris was in 1939; the last execution that ever took place was in the courtyard of the Paris prison of la Santé in 1977.

This little street is also lined with many pleasant cafés and tea-rooms, that is if you have any appetite left!

➤ Nearest metro Odéon.

One Ruler Replaces Another!

At the end of the wall, under the arcades at 36 rue de Vaugirard, very near the Luxembourg Palace, is the Paris standard metre. This unit of measure was adopted by the French on August 1st 1793, not long after Louis XVI was beheaded. The metre is one ten millionth of the meridian arc between the North Pole and the equator.

Until this time, units of measure varied from region to region in France. The metric system, revolutionary in spirit as it was common to all, caused great confusion amongst the illiterate. Dividing between 2, 4, or 8 had been easy, because any piece of string could be folded in half or into thirds, but to find a fraction of a metre was immeasurably difficult.

The Mire du Sud

The mire is a stone marker or bollard situated in the parc Montsouris, near the boulevard Jourdan entrance. It measures 4 metres and is pierced with a small occulus. The name of Napoleon was removed during the Restoration, and a large groove is visible where it was chiselled out.

The mire marks the original Paris meridian, a straight line starting here and running through the centre of the Paris Observatory. It joins Dunkerque and Perpignan, passing via the mire du nord in Montmartre. The Greenwich meridian was not adopted until 1884.

To commemorate work done on the meridian by François Arago, France commissioned a work in Paris by the Dutch sculptor Jan Dibbets. This imaginative sculpture consists of over a 100 circular medallions dotted along the meridian line. The first one is located by the mire. Each medallion bears the name Arago and has arrows marking the direction of the line. This work replaces the original statue of Arago, once located at the Observatory, which was melted down by the Germans during the Occupation.

La Monnaie (The Paris Mint)

The Mint of Paris was built during the reign of Louis XV. It is open as a museum and the story of coins can be traced from their origins to the present day. The huge presses in which coins were struck are on display, and medals are still made here today.

In the courtyard of the museum another Gnomon can be seen. It is a vertical meridian in the form of an obelisk like the one at St Sulpice. Its face is engraved with the 12 signs of the zodiac. The overall height of the obelisk is just under 8 metres. The meridian was calculated by a priest called Pingré who had abandoned the church to persue his passion for astronomy in 1745. The vertical meridian can be seen in the courtyard of the mint when the museum is open.

➤ **Hotel de la Monnaie, 11 quai de Conti, 75006, nearest metro Pont-Neuf.**

Pantheon and Foucault's Pendulum

It is an honour to be buried in this church which has become a monument to France's greatest men. The building is open as a museum and Foucault's pendulum hangs here. (The pendulum inspired a best selling thriller by Umberto Ecco.)

Foucault was a brilliant scientist who specialised in optics. He invented the machine named after him that enabled lens makers to measure focal length precisely. Foucault was determined to demonstrate publicly that the earth rotated. His idea was simple and brilliant. He suspended his pendulum from the dome at some 200 feet. The pendulum has a fine needle point at its base that drags in a sand pit leaving the trace of its passage. Foucault was able to demonstrate that the pendulum was stationary and that the earth was rotating. As Dan Brown reminds us, people who had challenged fixed ideas about the universe had been burnt as heritics in the past. From the age of Enlightenment onwards, even the Church had opened its mind towards scientific discovery.

Pont des St Pères

There are over 30 bridges in Paris and each one has a story to tell. The pont des St Pères is where the police catch up with the truck containing the soap bar in which Langdon's GPS dot is hidden. If you ever find this bridge in Paris, please let us know where it is.

The Church of St Médard

The church is located at the bottom end of the lively and bustling market street rue Mouffetard. This lovely church is dedicated to the patron saint of umbrella makers!

In the small cemetery of the church, a strange sect gathered regularly around the tomb of a churchman called François Pâris. Reports of miraculous cures spread rapidly, and the members of the sect, called the "Convulsionists", would go into trances. The ever increasing crowds went into a frenzy of collective hysteria. The alarming situation was brought to a sudden end when the church closed the cemetery, and pinned a notice in the entrance saying, "The king hereby forebids God to perform miracles in this place!"

➤ **Nearest metro Censier-Daubenton.**

Mitterrand "the Sphinx" and his Grands Travaux

François Mitterrand was president of France for 14 years, from 1981 to 1995. Dan Brown says that he is called the Sphinx in France. He was charicatured as a Sphinx in several leading French newspapers. The name does not derive solely from the Pyramid at the Louvre, but from the pharaoh-like nature of his building plan for Paris. Mitterrand's master plan for the city is referred to as his "Grands Travaux". It changed the face of Paris in the 20th century as Haussmann had done in the 19th.

During the 80s and early 90s, Paris became a huge building site with projects stretching along the Seine from east to west. Monuments such as the Louvre were restored, others were reused such as the Orsay Railway Station, and the peripheral areas of Paris were developed from Bercy to la Défense.

Mitterrand is thought to have been a freemason, member of the Grand Orient Lodge. He also seems to have had dealings with the modern Priory of Sion leader Pierre Plantard de Saint Clair. His visit to Rennes-le-Château before his election was well publicised in France!

The president frequently consulted a famous French astrologer Elizabeth Tessier, whose job was to calculate auspicious days for his important decisions.

THE MAJOR BUILDINGS OF MITTERRAND'S MASTER PLAN FOR PARIS FROM EAST TO WEST:

- **Bercy:** Ministry of Finance and picturesque wine village. To visit the delightfully renovated wine village go to metro Cour-St Émilion. Bercy Sports Stadium, pyramid shaped of course, seats up to 17,000.

- **The New Bibiothèque nationale:** Four 80 metre towers symbolise open books. Metro Quai de la Gare.

- **The New Opera House** at la Bastille.

- **The Institute of the Arab World**, 11, quai St-Bernard. Roof-top tearoom with unbeatable views of Notre Dame. Metro Jussieu.

- **The Louvre with its Pyramid Complex**, metro Palais-Royal-Musée-du-Louvre.

- **Complete Refurbishment of the Champs-Élysées**, metro Georges-V or Étoile.

- **The Grande Arche of la Défense**, metro Grande-Arche-de-la-Défense. Panoramic lift to roof-top for superb views of Paris. The roof-top terrace is a mosaic of the zodiac called "Map of the Sky".

Beneath The Rose Line

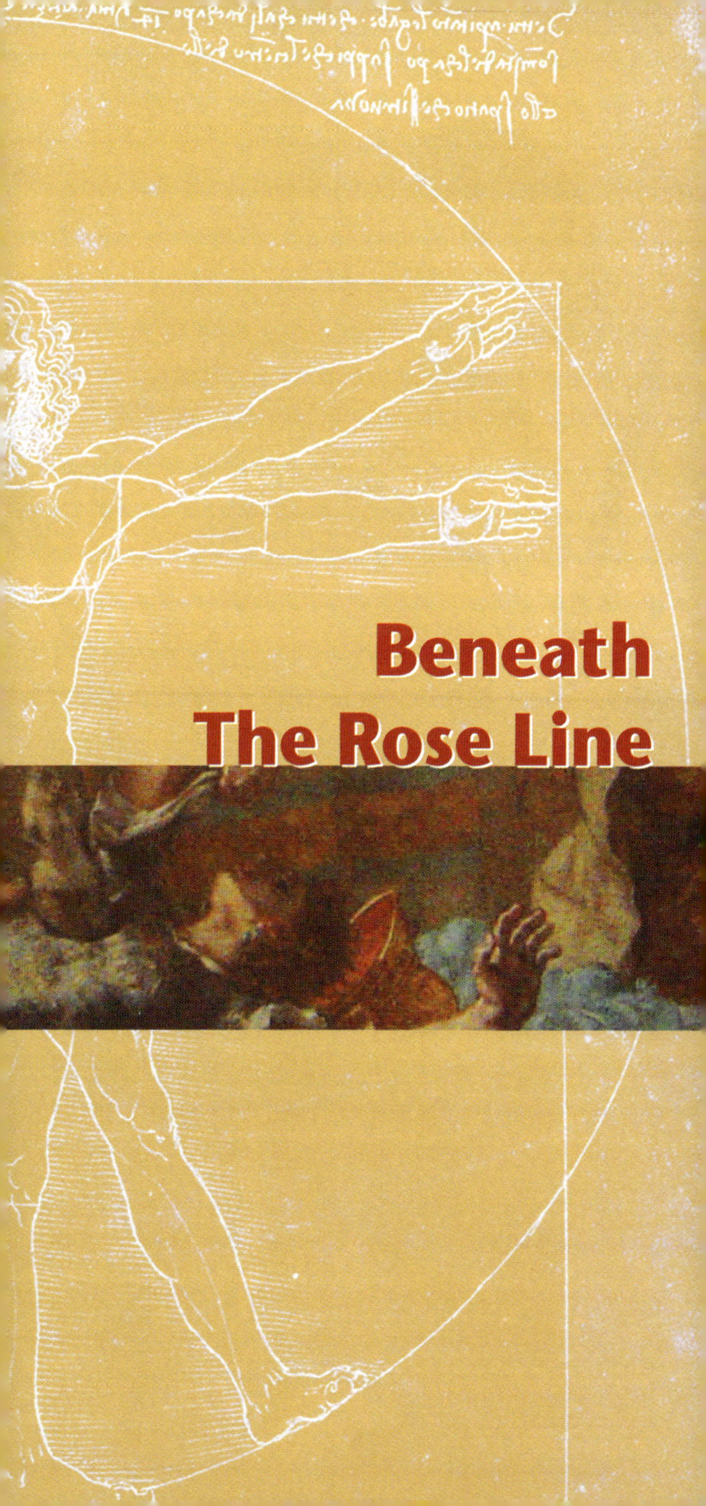

St Sulpice Church R.R.

The Story of Saint Sulpice The Key to the Quest for the Holy Grail

Two Mysterious Saunières

St Sulpice is inextricably linked to the mystery of the Holy Grail. A string of endless leads bring researchers back to this church.

The mystery begins when the real life Saunière, humble parish priest of Rennes-le-Château, found strange coded documents hidden in the pillar of an altar of his church.

He showed them to the Bishop of Carcassone, who instructed Saunière to take the documents to St Sulpice. He spent about three weeks there before returning to Rennes-le-Château where he then, suddenly and inexplicably, had inexaustible funds at his disposal. No one has been able to explain his sudden and new found wealth, although it has been attributed to both alchemy and the illicit selling of mass. He built a costly road to his church which was renovated, he built a mansion, that he named Villa Béthanie, and a fortified tower to contain his ever growing library. Coincidently Béthanie was the name of the Arch or Motherhouse of the Priory of Sion.

Saunière had the inscription "Terribilis est locus iste" or "Dreadful is this place" painted over the porch to his church, which as will be shown, is another link with

St Sulpice. The second Saunière is, of course, Dan Brown's murdered curator of the Louvre. Saunière from Rennes-le-Château died mysteriously on January the 17th, the saint's day of St Sulpice.

SS Saint Sulpice and SS Secret Society!

A secret society known as the Compagnie du St Sacrement had its centre of operations at St Sulpice, and the Priory of Sion are said to be the power behind both this group and the Knights Templars. There was an actual Abbot named Bieil here at the end of the 19th century. It is highly likely that he met and had dealings with the priest Saunière, and it is suggested that their dealings were over the hidden treasure.

Bieil is the name Brown gives the nun who lives here and acts as the guardian of the Priory's treasure.

The meridian line and the Gnomon, central to *The Da Vinci Code* are located in the church, ➤ **See under Gnomon** (no pun intended) for a synopsis of the principal events!

What Great Mystery This St Sulpice

Although only a parish church, St Sulpice was a hugely ambitious project built on a scale that matches that of the Cathedral of Paris. The ground plan of St Sulpice is just 17 metres less than Notre Dame, but is 10 metres wider. The stone vaults of the two are nearly identical, soaring above the heads of the congregation at some 35 metres.

A Red Snake

An extraordinary document known as the "Serpent Rouge" or "Red Snake" is kept at the Bibliothèque nationale. It forms part of the famous "Dossiers secrets" upon which the theories in *The Da Vinci Code* are based. This document is believed to be written by four men including Jean Cocteau, one of the Grand Masters of the Priory of Sion. Amongst various enigmatic texts, such as a *genealogy of the Merovingians* and a series of poems relating to the signs of the zodiac, it also includes a ground plan of St Sulpice Church! One of the poems eulogises, "Isis queen of all sources benevolent." Isis, the Egyptian Mother Goddess, is a heroine in the story (➤ **See p. 59 and Louvre**). As will be revealed, Isis has both a mysterious link with St Sulpice and with Paris in general. According to this text, the mother goddess Isis is not the Virgin Mary, but Mary Magdalene, mother of all churches. This document reinforces the notion that Mary Magdalene did become a mother. The presence of the genealogy of the Merovingians supports the idea that the authors of the document, who's protectors were at St Sulpice, believed that the Merovingian kings were the direct descendants of this Mother Mary. The red snake itself symbolises the blood line. There seems to be strong evidence that someone wished to supress the document and the ideas it was perpetuating. The three other men associated with producing it were all found hanged in March 1967. Was this the work of another Silas?

Ancient Origins and a Pagan Past

The origins of St Sulpice date back to the 12th century, when as a dependance of the Abbey of St Germain-des-Prés, the church was dedicated to St Sulpicius, a 6th century Bishop of Bourges, unsurprisingly of the Merovingian era. Brown says that a pagan temple dedicated to Isis stood on this ground, and it is also argued that the celtic founders of the city, "the Parisii" took their name from their veneration of Isis. There is plenty of evidence for the many pagan shrines on the left bank, dating from the Gallo-Roman period, and maps and drawings from the past, do show the existence of this temple, although it was probably closer to St Germain-des-Prés.

Great Wealth for Rebuilding

The church of today is part 17th and part 18th century, and was built as a result of this area suddenly becoming a desirable residential quarter. As Louis XIV prepared to move his court to Versailles, the city naturally spread towards the south-west. Many bridges were built across the Seine to give easier access, and the nobility began to build beautiful mansions on this side of the river. With a new congregation of wealthy benefactors, it became both possible and necessary to rebuild the old church. Anne of Austria, Louis XIV's mother, laid the first stone of the new church on the February 20th 1646.

Where did the money come from?

There is, however, perhaps a more sinister explanation for the sudden injection of capital into the rebuilding of the church. It has already been mentioned that the Compagnie du St Sacrement, a secret society, supposedly empowered by the Priory of Sion, had its centre of operations here. They were founded shortly before the rebuilding of the church began, between 1627 and 1629. The men associated with this group include the king's brother, Gaston d'Orleans, Charles Fouquet, the brother of Louis XIV's Superintendent of Finances, St Vincent de Paul, the Bishop of Alet (a town incidently near Rennes-le-Château) and Jean-Jacques Olier, the founder of the Seminary of St Sulpice!

Six Architects in 143 Years

This new church was never completed but it stands today as a witness of the architectural audacity and daring of the period. The new style used, was both ambitious and remarkable; a catalyst that revolutionised the future of Parisian architecture, marking its move towards classicism. The project progressed slowly, troubled by uprisings, (la Fronde) war and financial difficulties. In the course of building, six different architects worked on the church over a period of 143 years!

Rebuilding began at the east end of the church (the location of the Lady Chapel and the altar) and work progressed slowly towards the west. After decades of problems, a competition was held in 1732 to find an architect capable of completing the church and its façade. The contract was won by an Italian architect called Giovanni Niccolo Servandoni. He was principally a theatre and stage designer, but had been trained in classical architecture in Florence. His plans were adopted, but when he died in 1766, the work was still incomplete. Servandoni died in a house he had designed next to the church, this can be seen at 6 place St Sulpice.

The Façade

From the far side of the square, the harmony between the proportions of the façade, the square and the fountain (19th century) is evident. The façade is both massive and imposing, even more so now that the triangular pediment, originally occupying the space between the two towers, has been demolished. The pediment would have lightened the structure, making it appear less squat than it does today.

Golden Numbers

Architects of the Ancient World used mysterious formulas to achieve perfection in their design. Dan Brown explains the use of two of these in his book, the Fibonacci sequence and the Golden Section. These numbers written by Saunière on the floor of the Louvre just before he dies, reveal the bank account number of his secret safety deposit box. Mathematicians have demonstrated how the Fibonacci sequence recurs in the most beautiful natural forms, from the perfectly geometrical nautilus shell, to the positioning of seeds in a sun flower head. It has been understood and used by man in both art and architecture. The sequence is infinite, where each number of the sequence is the sum of the two that proceed it, i.e. 1 + 1 = 2, 1 + 2 = 3, 2 + 3 = 5, 3 + 5 = 8 the sequence being 1, 1, 2, 3, 5, 8, etc. The increments of the sequence are related to the golden ratio, in that, over and above three, the relationship between any two numbers is 1.618 or that of the golden number. This relationship was discovered by the mathematician Robert Simson in the 1750s.

Divine Proportions

The Ancients were aware of the Golden Number (called Φ in Greek) and exploited it to create harmonious architectural

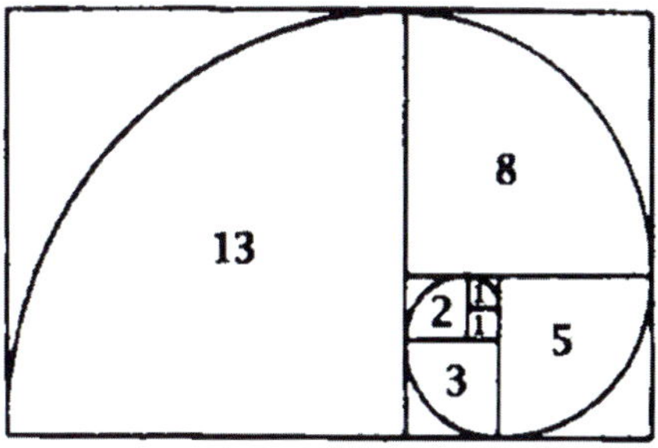

forms. The visual satisfaction achieved through its use, combined with the unexplainable nature of the number, led Renaissance theorists to believe it was divine. Luca Paciola, a friend of Da Vinci, wrote a treatise called *De Divina Proportione* in 1479. This treatise attempts to explain the number, but its title alludes to a belief that this perfection has its source in something far greater than man. The proportion renders a visually satisfying rectangle such as the post card or credit card. We see this relationship in ordinary every day objects around us, both natural and man made, and also in architecture, ranging from the ancient Greek temples to the great classical churches, and the modernist constructions of architects such as Le Corbusier. Many artists including Leonardo have structured their paintings using this formula. Servandoni would certainly have been aware of this.

Doric, Ionic and Corinthian

Servandoni's design at St Sulpice translates the gothic forms of Notre Dame into a classical two story portico, flanked by towers. As at Notre Dame, there are three levels of elevation, three portals and two bell towers. At St Sulpice, the cathedral portals with their high pointed gables are arched by semi circular vaults. The rose window of Notre Dame becomes an Italianate loggia or balcony closed in by a colonnade of triumphal arches.

The Rose symbolises the Virgin Mary, and therefore each cathedral dedicated to Notre Dame has one. The lack of such a window, may suggest that here, it is the Mother Goddess Mary Magdalene rather than the Virgin Mary, that was considered the more important. This would certainly concur with the arguments in *The Da Vinci Code*. The massive square towers of Notre Dame have been transformed, into circular drums topped with balustrades.

The three storeys of the façade follow the classical system of architectural orders: Doric, Ionic and Corinthian. The lower level columns are Doric, taking their name from the Greek word meaning rustic. They are the simplest form, grooved and slightly tapered towards the capitals on which lies the entablature. The entablature forms an unbroken horizontal line that optically reduces the verticality of the church and harmonizes the relation between its height and width. Classical architecture aims to create a balanced and harmonious structure, and each element is carefully calculated to play an important part in the whole. The second level consists of Ionic columns, again grooved but ending in scrolls. Originally, the arcaded loggia at this level was planned to be glassed in, to become an enormous library for the church.

Secret Dossiers and St Sulpice

Evidently, the church had a large library of books and documents, and it is thought that the elusive Compagnie du St Sacrement kept their archives here. The group was to meet a similar fate to the Knights Templars. They were threatened with excommunication by the Bishop of Tours, and charged with impious practices in 1651. Eventually, threatened by Louis XIV in 1665, the Compagnie recalled and concealed all its documents, which were hidden in a secret depository, thought to be the library of St Sulpice. A further literary link between the church and the Priory of Sion is Victor Hugo. He was married here in 1822 and is named as being Grand Master of the Priory between 1844-1885. Both Baudelaire and the infamous Marquis de Sade were baptised here! The man listed as succeding Cocteau as Grand Master of the Priory trained in the seminary here.

Modernism with a capital M (MM!)

This church has a long and complex association with controversial religious thinkers and scholars. In the 19th century, scholars began to apply modernist techniques to biblical scholarship; these looked at the Bible with a new critical methodology. One of the most famous of these was the French writer Ernest Renan who wrote a controversial *Life of Jesus*. At first, the church embraced this study, but soon realised that the Bible could not stand up to the kind of analysis used by this new breed of historian. A conflict ensued and the Modernists were soon seen as heretics. One particularly strong voice amongst this group belonged to Jean-Baptiste Hogan, unsurprisingly the director of the Seminary of St Sulpice between 1852-1884!

The Two Towers! Home of Angels and Kestrels

The two towers are decorated with double pairs of Corinthian columns. The right hand or south tower, which is incomplete, is interesting because it leaves lots of clues as to how the original builders went about constructing the church. The tower is dotted with small hollow cavities that the builders used to plug in their scaffolding. These can be seen on nearly all churches. Sometimes the holes have been plastered in to leave a smooth surface, but here, like at Notre Dame, they are used even today for maintenace work, and so remain visible. On either side of the main opening on the tower there are pillasters (square pillars). These have not been completed, and where the capitals should be, there are large bare blocks of stone that protrude, waiting to be carved into acanthus leaves. It can be deduced that the fine details of carving and sculpture were put onto the building *in situ* by an artist working high on his scaffold. Kestrels nest in the north tower of the church, and there is also a sculptor's studio. The resident artist specialises in carving angels.

The Sacred Tetragrammaton

The front of the North tower is decorated with a triangular tympanum, which in turn is carved with the Hebrew Tetragrammaton. It is made up of the letters YHWH and represents the never spoken Jewish name of God, which

יהוה

Jews are forbidden to say, to guard against desecration of the Sacred Name. In *The Da Vinci Code*, Dan Brown says this name is made up from an androgynous physical union between the masculine *Jah* and the feminine pre-hebraic name for Eve, *Havah*. He explains that for the ancient Jews, God was seen as having a powerful female counterpart referred to as Shekinah. The Shekinah is also known as the Sabath Bride or Sophia (*Chokmah* in Hebrew), the Goddess of Wisdom. Shekinah symbolises the presence of God and relates to a feminine aspect of the Holy Trinity. It is used to describe the visible manifestation of the divine presence, and is, in fact, another way of referring to God without using his name, for example as God appears to Moses in the burning bush. The Sacred Tetragrammaton is pronounced as *adonai* meaning "the Lord" or simply *ha shem* meaning "the name". This Hebrew inscription is curiously inexplicable on a Christian church. The Tetragrammaton, meaning four letters, is ancient and appears in the Dead Sea Scrolls that are over 2000 years old. Langdon lectures on this to his students.

The Porch

It is here that Silas bangs three times on the door in the dead of night, to wake up Sandrine Bieil. Standing in the massive porch, he decides to leave his gun behind, thinking it has no place in a house of God. Later, when he murders Bieil, he uses a weapon that the church provides, one of the enormous candlesticks from the altar. As he prepares to enter the church, he believes, without a doubt, that he will soon have the map that will lead his superiors to the location of the secret that will save Opus Dei.

The porch is massive, its width and height seem to dwarf anyone who enters it. The interior is sculpted with 7 low relief panels, illustrating the three theoligical virtues (Faith, Hope and Charity) and the four cardinal virtues (Truth, Fortitude, Temperance and Prudence.) They are the work of two brothers called Slodtz, whose work can be seen elsewhere in Paris including the Church of St Merry.

A Pagan Inscription and a Sumptuous Dinner

Above the central portal, a faded and enigmatic inscription reads, "Le peuple français reconnoit l'Etre suprême et

l'immortalité de l'ame." This translates as, "The French Nation believes in the Supreme Being and the immortality of the soul." The inscription dates back to the French Revolution when under Robespierre many churches were reopened as pagan temples and used for secular activities. Napoleon once held a banquet here for 750 guests, as part of his celebrations on his return from the Egyptian Campaign.

Inside the church

Windows

Inside the church, in the stained-glass window of the north transept, are the intertwined initials P and S. The church maintains that these refer to St Peter and not the Priory of Sion!

Crypt

There is a crypt beneath the church where about 5,000 people were buried between 1743-1793. Huge trapdoors behind the high alter in the choir were used to lower the bodies down into this underground burial chamber. It is said by the church that the revolutionary leader Saint-Just, used to hold secret meetings there.

The Gnomon

Silas's role at the church centres around the fascinating Gnomon. The Gnomon derives its name from an ancient

Greek word that means indicator, and it is the correct name for the pointer that casts a shadow on a sundial. It is often used to refer to the sundial itself. The Gnomon is located in the transept of the building, and runs north south directly in front of the main altar.

Murder in the Cathedral

In *The Da Vinci Code* Silas has come here for one reason only, to look for the keystone. He has been told that it will lead him to the ultimate treasure. As each of the Priory of Sion Masters concurs with their instructions, he eliminates them, and then comes to the church to seek his treasure. Silas has been told that the coveted keystone lies beneath the Rose Line at the base of the St Sulpice obelisk. Silas does not realise that he has been tricked.

Sandrine Bieil, guardian of the church, knows that if anyone comes looking for the treasure here, they have infiltrated the innermost ring of the Priory members. She must immediately sound the alert. Silas breaks the floor panel concealing the keystone, and finds a tablet containing the disappointing inscription: "Job 38:11". He goes to the great Bible on the altar to read the appropriate passage, and this is when he realises he has been duped. The passage reads, "Hitherto shalt thou come, but no further." The consequences are terrible. The murders he has commited mean that the secret is lost forever. In a frenzy of rage, the monk discovers Sister Bieil at the phone giving the alert. He uses the candlestick, still in his hand, to carry out her murder.

A Moveable Feast

For the purposes of the story, and undoubtedly for dramatic effect, Dan Brown says that the Gnomon is a vestige of the pagan temple that once stood here. Although such an instrument can be construed as pagan, it has both a theological and scientific purpose: An extremely accurate sundial used to calculate the dates of moveable feasts, such as Easter. It also enabled the astronomer Le Monnier to perfect his observations of the movement of the sun and to study the obliquity of the ecliptic. Many churches were used by scientists for their experiments. Foucault's pendulum is in the nearby Pantheon, and the enigmatic tour St Jacques was used by Pascal for perfecting his barometer.

The existing Gnomon was designed by the astronomer Charles Le Monnier. In 1743, he employed the chief engineer of the Louvre, Claude Lanois, to trace out the meridian line. The original idea dated back to 1727, when a Parisian clockmaker decided to create an accurate system by which to set the clocks of Paris.

Markings from this original Gnomon can still be seen on the floor just inside the south transept portal.

The existing meridian line, inlaid in brass, is referred to by Brown as the Rose Line. The term is used to refer to the cardinal points in a compass rose. The Priory of Sion documents do refer to such a line, and the main locations of *The Da Vinci Code* fall on the meridian that runs through St Sulpice and the Louvre. Brown also assimilates Rose Line with Rosslyn to lead the treasure hunt of his heroes to the chapel of the same name in Scotland, the Rosslyn Chapel or the chapel of codes.

Mignonne, allons voir si la rose...

In *The Da Vinci Code* the rose is an extremely important symbol. Teabing and Langdon explain to Sophie how the rose came to reinforce the notion of Mary Magdalene having produced a blood line with Christ. The five petaled rose is like the pentacle of Venus, the goddess of love. We are also told that rose, the same word used in many languages, is also an anagram of Eros! The rose symbolises Mary Magdalene, whose relics are in fact the Holy Grail, and therefore the Rose Line becomes an appropriate indicator or key to the hiding place of this holy secret.

Tempus Fugit

The Gnomon still works but does not function correctly because part of its optical system is now missing. The sundial consists of two lenses in the upper window of the south transept, and a marble obelisk in the north. The two are linked together by a brass line inlaid into the floor of the church, which is a true north-south meridian. In the floor of the south transept, a carved panel indicates the beginning of the meridian. The meridian ends at the summit of the obelisk, its central point, more or less in front of the main altar, is marked by an oval brass plaque.

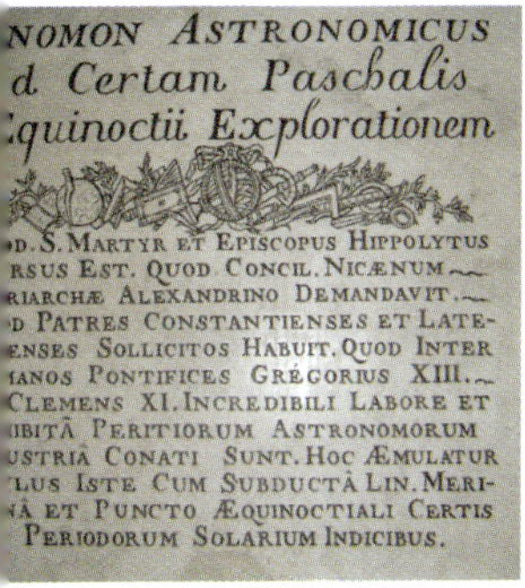

During the spring and autumn equinoxes, when the sun is at its zenith and the days and nights are of equal length, the oval plaque is illuminated at midday.

During the winter solstice, when the sun is at its lowest at midday, the light ray falls on the marker of the obelisk.

During the summer solstice, when the sun is at its highest, the south transept floor plaque is illuminated.

Originally the south transept window containing the two lenses was blanked out to reduce light interference. The metal blackout was replaced with leaded glass in 1866. This means that nowadays it is difficult to take clear readings from the Gnomon.

The obelisk, designed by Servandoni, is made from marble and is topped with an orb and cross. Its total height is 10.72m. The astrological symbol of capricorn ♑ is engraved towards the top. This marks the winter solstice on the 21st of December. Below, on the left side of the brass meridian line is the sign of sagitarius ♐, and on the right side, the sign of aquarius ♋. These do not have mystical or astrological significance, but are astronomical and denote respectively where the sun marks the 21st of January and the 21st of November.

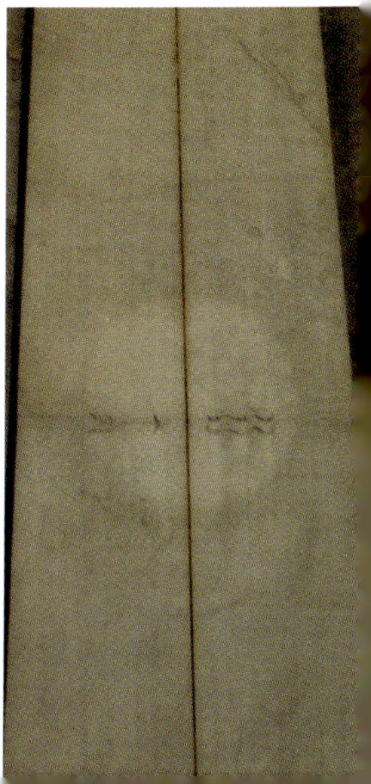

The engraved images and texts below give explanations of both the scientific and theological use of the Gnomon. The plinth is engraved on the left side with an array of intertwined scientific instruments, and on the right, with a lamb carrying a cross.

The scientific instruments speak for themselves, while the lamb is a reminder of Christian sacrifice. Since ancient times, the lamb has symbolised the regenerational power of spring, innocence, purity and new life. Because it is highly prized, it has often been a principal sacrificial victim. At Easter, it has represented the sacrificial death and resurrection of Christ. John the Baptist, when he first saw Christ said, "Behold the lamb of God, which taketh away the sin of the world" (John 1:29).

The lamb in the Apocalypse, carrying the book of the seven seals, is Christ as judge at the second coming. As the good shepherd, Christ cares for his flock and rescues the lost lamb that has gone astray. Here, the lamb specifically relates to the Gnomon's use by the church for calculating the date of Easter, which falls on the first Sunday after the first full moon that follows the spring equinox. The inscriptions that have been chiseled out referred to the king and his ministers. This was done during the Revolution.

The inscription, "Quid Mihi est in Coelo", reflects the Churche's use of science. It translates as, "What should I seek in the sky, and what should I desire on earth other than you Lord, you are the God of my heart and the heritage I desire."

The Chapel of the Holy Angels and Delacroix

Terribilis est locus iste

The Chapel des Saints-Anges is the first in a series that run along the south side aisle. It was decorated by Delacroix between 1861 and 1863, the date that he died. Delacroix, enthusiastic about this project, took a studio near the church; it is now a museum. The paintings have their source in both the Old Testament and the biblical apocrypha. Since they have been known, the latter books became the source for a rich and complex system of images and symbols that became powerful tools for artists.

The ceiling painting shows St Michael. In Revelations, he is described as the principal fighter in the heavenly battle, casting out the great dragon, and is responsible for the fall of the rebel angel. (Revelations 12: 7-9) Because his role is primarily military, he is revered by kings and is the patron of knights, soldiers and armourers. Louis XI founded an order of St Michael, Francis I was given Raphael's painting (now in the Louvre) which inspired Delacroix's work here. The order of St Michael symbolised the union of the king and the church. In the book of Daniel it is said that Michael is the protector of Jacob. Here he watches over his protegé below.

On the east wall of the chapel is the story of Jacob, taken from Genesis 25-37 and 42-50. In his novel *The Nights of Lutetia*, David Shahar shows that he believes that the painting has a hidden purpose: the picture symbolizes the birth of Israel, but it is not clear exactly who Jacob is fighting.

Another curious link exists here with Saunière from Rennes-le-Château, who had the inscription "Terribilis est locus iste" painted above the porch to his church. This comes from Genesis 28:17, "How dreadful is this place." It is what Jacob says after his dream of the ladder and before naming the spot Bethel.

A Remorseful Thief

Jacob, the younger twin, aided by his mother, tricks his brother Esau out of his inheritance. To avoid the wrath of Esau, Jacob spends years in exile. On his return to make peace with his brother, Jacob was attacked in the night. Jacob fought all night with a man who refused to reveal his identity. At daybreak, he is told he is to be called *Israel*, which means "ruling with god". His only wound was a blow to the hip that left him with a limp. At daybreak, Jacob perceives he has been fighting with God.

In the painting, Delacroix draws attention to the immense struggle that Jacob undergoes; every muscle of his body is

exaggerated and this is juxtaposed with the calm, statue-like quality of the angel. The painting partly, symbolises mankind's struggle with the upholding of his own religious ideals. The background and the forest are painted with a quick, light and feathery brushtroke. He was criticised for this but it is an undeniable step towards Impressionism. In the foreground, bottom right, there is a small separate still life. He is said to have painted this in just twenty minutes. Jacob's cloak, arrows, and quiver are represented, as is his straw hat. The hat is far more likely to have been worn by Delacroix himself, than Jacob!

A Repentant Sinner

On the west wall, the artist has painted the story of Heliodorus, taken from the second book of Maccabees. The

pagan Heliodorus has been sent to sack the Temple, but in doing so, he is struck down by an angel on horseback and dies. The Christians pray for his soul, he is then ressucitated, repents and converts to Christianity. This painting is a wonderful vehicle through which Delacroix can exploit his favourite themes: rich oriental colour, textures, jewels, and a horse set against a background of baroque movement. This painting typifies romantic ardour, for which the artist is famous.

If Music be the Food of Love…

The organ of St Sulpice is considered one of the finest in the world. After having been restored in the 19th century it was reinaugurated. The greatest composers of the day were present, including, Saint-Saëns, Cherubini, Rossini and César Franck. Some of the finest music ever written, including that of Mozart, is shown to follow the rules of the Golden Number. Mozart, Beethoven and Gershwin were all prominent freemasons according to Brown.

➤ **Delacroix Museum, 6, rue Furstenberg, 75006. 01 44 41 86 50. Metro St Germain-des-Prés (last home and studio of the artist). 9.30am-5pm. Closed Tuesdays.**
There are regular organ concerts at St Sulpice.

Under the Pyramids

The Louvre Pyramid

A Guided *Da Vinci Code* Tour of the Louvre

The following chapter is a guided *Da Vinci Code* tour of the Louvre. The proposed circuit covers some of the most famous works in the museum that are included in the book, but also some "off the beaten track" works that illustrate the themes that are evoked in the story. The circuit should take about two hours, but can be prolonged or shortened depending on whether you hurry or linger.

Exterior

Dan Brown mentions the massive size of the Louvre, which is made up of some 8 miles of corridors, and to walk the whole perimeter is a three mile journey. The building itself since, 1993, one of the largest museums in the world, has been built up over centuries.

Each part of the building echoes art and architecture from differing historical periods. The earliest part of the museum you see is the lovely Renaissance "Cour carrée", the most recent is the Pyramid. A variety of architectural periods between the two are represented, but the oldest part, the original medieval castle, can only be seen from inside.

Although many traditionalists do not like the modern Pyramid, it is appropriate that the museum building, an art historical manifesto in itself, should also represent the architecture of our own day and age.

The architect I. M. Pei chose the pyramid for several reasons, but primarily he needed to be able to bring light into the underground system of corridors he had designed. This is one of the reasons for the success of his project. Other architects had simply proposed making the unwieldy building bigger. I. M. Pei proposed a labyrinth of underground corridors that simplified access to all parts of the museum.

The pyramid has ancient and iconic status in the world of art history and the glass and metallic structure called a "verrière" is a traditional Parisian architectural type. I. M. Pei pays tribute to this.

There is direct access to the Louvre from the metro station "Palais-Royal – Musée-du-Louvre" on line n° 1. Leave the metro and follow the platform signs "Musée du Louvre". This will lead you via the shopping mall "Carrousel du Louvre" to the inverted pyramid. You will pass toilet facilities and a large fast food cafeteria.

The Tourist Office is located near the inverted pyramid. There are security bag checks at this point. As you head towards the main pyramid where tickets can be purchased, you pass a post office and the museum's own shops, selling reproductions, museum gifts and a large book shop specialising in the history of art (many titles are available in English). Bag check-in and cloak rooms are only available once you have purchased your ticket. The museum pass is valid here and well worth purchasing if you are visiting several museums over a few days (➤ **See The Keystone Chapter for more information**).

Beneath the Pyramid

The pyramid complex was opened in 1989 to coincide with the bicentenary of the French Revolution. The renovation of the Richelieu Wing, adding 165 galleries and exhibiting some 12,000 works was opened in 1993, celebrating the bicentenary of the museum.

The Louvre Pyramid is designed according to the proportions of the great pyramid at Ghiza in Egypt. The pyramid shape is supposed to have magic powers, it is said that food kept under this shape will keep longer, and a razor kept under the perfect pyramidal form will never go blunt. Unfortunately due to strict security nowadays you cannot test this, as neither food nor razors are allowed in the museum!

The glass structure was made by the French company St Gobain, who also made the mirrors in the famed Hall of Mirrors in Versailles. It is made of pure white sand from Fontainebleau, laminated in France, and polished in England. How many panes of glass? Dan Brown says 666, the number of the devil, which is great fun (➤ **See Seven

Seals for the symbolism of this). The author of this guide calculates 603 lozenges and 70 triangles. No two sources seem to agree and there has been much ink spilled over this, but perhaps it does not really matter!

The creamy coloured stone comes from the famous Burgundian quarries at Comblanchien. A special concrete was designed to match the colour of the stone exactly. The concrete was shuttered using special fine grained pine from Oregon that was oiled and waxed to give a perfectly smooth finish while maintaining the wood grain.

From the pyramid complex, access can be gained to the three wings of the Louvre: Richelieu to the north, Sully to the east and Denon to the south. This tour follows a route through Sully and Denon returning to the starting point.

The entrance ticket is valid all day and you can leave the museum for a break and return later to take in the Richelieu Wing.

The Tour Starts Here

Warning! The museum is often obliged to move works for one reason or another (maintenance, restauration or for purposes of loan). Pick up the free map-guide from the information rotunda beneath the Pyramid.

Begin the tour by following the Sully Wing entrance, and go up the small escalator. At the top, pass the souvenir boutique, under a mini-pyramid, and continue to the ticket check. Go straight ahead till you come to the medieval Louvre. Just before you enter the spectacular moat, there is a model of the castle and keep (in the wall to the left). Walk straight on through the moat. The original Louvre was built by King Philip Augustus in the 1180s, to defend Paris from the English while the king was away on crusade. The foundations of the castle were discovered and restored between 1984-85. Turn right, following the moat at the **corner tower**. This tower is carved with many **hearts**, which are the original medieval masons' marks. Continue through the moat, pass **two towers** on your right, these guard the main entrance into the fortress. A draw-bridge, at modern day ceiling level, crossed from the castle to the city wall on your left-hand side. Carry straight on, climb the stairs and stop at the ***Great Sphinx of Tanis***.

The *Sphinx of Tanis*

Dan Brown's heroes follow a path coded by symbols from the ancient world. Saunière, curator of the Louvre, collects these symbols, especially the Egyptian ankh. This symbolises the breath of life, and in Egyptian art, ankh can be seen held at the nose of Pharaohes by the gods. The nose was considered the seat of life by which a magic force entered the body. Invaders later smashed the *Sphinx's* nose to symbolicaly take the statues life. The *Sphinx* is made from one block of pink granite, which comes from Aswan in Southern Egypt, but it was found at the delta of the Nile in the north. It weighs 28 tons and was moved using manpower; one man could pull one ton. It was brought to France by boat and the museum had to pierce a hole in the wall to put the *Sphinx* in place. It guards the entrance to the Egyptian collections, and is about 4000 years old.

Take the stairs to your right.

Venus de Milo

This is an emblematic work at the Louvre. The statue should really be called Aphrodite as she is Greek and not Roman. Her name comes from the Cycladic Island where she was found, "Melos", which became Milo in French. The name of the island means apple and it is thought she may have been holding an apple in her hand. The link between the Sacred Feminine and the apple is clearly explained in *The Da Vinci Code* and apple is the word that opens the final cryptex (➤ **See also under symbols**).

Venus is thought to be late 2nd or early 3rd century BC. Walk along the gallery to take a look at the statue from a distance. The position she holds is called "contraposto": her head is slightly turned, with her shoulders tilted at an angle opposite to the one made by the line of her hips, and one leg moves forward.

The right side of her body forms a straight line, the left an S-like curve.

This position, considered life-like and elegant is used repeatedly by artists through the ages, and some medieval representations of the Virgin follow this pattern. Later you will see a Mary Magdalene which is inspired by classical Greek sculpture.

Continue along the gallery of Greek antiquities, turn left into the last room, number 7.

Parthenon Frieze

On the far end wall of the gallery is a fragment of the frieze from the Parthenon Temple on the Athens Acropolis. The frieze formed a continuous band around the top of the building and represented one of the most important annual celebrations of the Sacred Feminine "Athena". Athena was the daughter of Zeus. She is the patron deity of war, and also

of many skills and crafts, and is often represented in her armour. Sometimes she has an owl on her shoulder. The procession on the frieze shows just eight out of the original 360 figures that progressed in a stately parade to deliver a woven tunic to the goddess. The solemnity of the occasion is captured in the rhythmic folds of the drapery and the elegant and dignified manner in which the figures stand.

The pattern of the procession is given lively interest by the two male figures who are masters of ceremony.

They face the opposite direction, turning towards the young virgins.

As you leave the sculpture, cross the main gallery into the Caryatid Ballroom (room n° 17).

Roman copies of Greek Statues: *Diana* and *Hermaphrodite*

When the Louvre was still a royal palace, this room was host to the wedding celebrations of the future King, Francis II and Mary Queen of Scots. This room is filled with Roman copies of Greek masterpieces.

Many of the original works were made in bronze, but the Romans copied them in marble. The bronze was melted down for use in warfare. Much of our knowledge of Greek art comes from Roman copies rather than the originals, which have been lost. In the middle of the room is the beautiful *Diana*, called the *Diana of Versailles*. She is goddess of the hunt and is associated with the night and therefore is wearing her attribute, the crescent moon, on her head.

At the far end of the room, tucked away in the right-hand corner, is a sleeping *Hermaphrodite*. From behind, the figure looks like a beautiful slumbering Venus; from in front her anatomy leaves no doubt that the figure represents a mythological union of blade and chalice, male and female. The large cushion she sleeps on was sculpted by Bernini in the 17th century. In mythology, the naiad Salmacis prayed that she and the son of Hermes and Aphrodite might be forever united. When she embraced him, their bodies were joined into one, becoming half man, half woman. Biblical Adam is like this until a rib is removed to create a separate female. Some of Da Vinci's figures share this same "androgynous" quality. Beside *Hermaphrodite* is a beautiful group representing the three Graces.

Leave the ball-room the way you entered, turn immediately right, then climb the magnificent staircase to *Winged Victory*.

Victory of Samothrace

The *Winged Victory* is another of the Louvre's emblematic goddess figures, one of the most inspired and grandiose of Greek works. The Ancients had no complex about using the female figure to symbolise military prowess. Originally the sculpture was painted in bright colours and would have been holding symbols of victory in each hand (probably the laurel wreath and, or a trumpet).

The figure, now headless and armless, was discovered in about 100 pieces. She is believed to commemorate a naval victory in about 200 BC. The ship's prow on which she stands is an original element of its theatrical staging. *Winged Victory* was on a clifftop overlooking the entrance to a harbour.

The grand staircase was built especially for her in the 1930s. Archaeologists found one of her hands in the 1950s, and her thumb is in a museum in Vienna.

Climb the steps left of *Victory* and turn immediately right. This takes you into the rotunda that gives access to the Apollo Gallery.

The Crown Jewels

The Apollo Gallery has just been restored, and is home to the collection of curiosities and antiquities that Louis XIV kept at Versailles. The crown jewels from the 17th to 19th century are on display here. The jewellery of the Merovingian Queen Aregonde is displayed in the Richelieu wing in the collection of "Medieval Objets d'art".

Leave the Apollo Gallery and turn immediately right. The 6th room, n° 30, is part of the Egyptian collection.

Isis and the Egyptians

Cross the room diagonally to the right, to find a beautiful collection of statuettes showing the goddess Isis (display cabinet n° 2). The theory that Teabing explains to Sophie is

Isis-Aphrodite

Isis

wonderfully illustrated here with a collection of small figurines representing Isis breastfeeding her son Horus.

Isis and her brother-husband, and their miraculously conceived son Horus make a Holy Trinity. Their story was retold by the Greeks and eventually by the Christians.

Osiris was murdered and cut into 14 pieces. Isis searched the length and breadth of the Nile and found 13 of the 14 parts, which she miraculously put back together. Not only are they a Holy Trinity but Osiris undergoes martyrdom, death and resurrection. Horus with a falcon's head can be seen to the left.

As you leave the room the way you came in, just to the right of the exit is an *Isis-Aphrodite*; the Egyptian goddess is shown as adopted and adapted by the Greeks (display cabinet n° 10). Compare the Greek *Isis-Aphrodite* with the Egyptian goddess next to her.

Walk back to the *Victory of Samothrace,* cross in front of her and climb the steps to rooms 1 then 2.

Botticelli (Grand Master of The Priory of Sion 1483-1510)

Botticelli is a nickname that means little barrel. The artist's real name was Alessandro Filipepi. He lived from about 1445-1510 and was seven years older than Leonardo Da Vinci. The painting in room 2 is a wall fresco from the Villa

Lemmi near Florence. It was probably commissioned to celebrate the wedding of Lorenzo Tornabuoni.

In room 1, his wife is presented to Venus and the three Graces in order to prepare for marriage. In room 2, her bridegroom is educated for married life. His education is illustrated by using the symbols of the Trivium and Quadrivium (➤ **See Chartres Cathedral p. 189**). A woman, representing grammar, leads him by the hand to the Trivium. He is presented to a meeting of the liberal arts. Once grammar is learnt, he progresses to the other literary subjects: dialectic holds a scorpion, rhetoric holds a scroll.

The meeting is presided over by Philosophy, who holds a long-bow in the form of a serpent. In the Quadrivium, Arithmetic holds an abacus, Geometry has a set-square, Astronomy has an astrolabe and Music is playing a portable organ, the bellows of which she is pumping with her left hand.

The grace, delicacy and linear draughtsmanship demonstrated here are typical of the Florentine school. Botticelli has created an atmosphere of melancholy. Comparing the style used here (linear and flat, like a collage), with the painting of Da Vinci, illustrates what was so special about Leonardo's life-like way of painting. His figures have an almost photographic reality and literally fit into the perspective of the background.

Continue on into room 3, the magnificent Salon carré.

In this room there are some very beautiful early Italian paintings. On the right as you enter, you will see Giotto's *St Francis*, the founder of the Franciscan order, receiving the Stigmata, which was painted around 1290. This was during the reign of Philip the Fair, shortly before the downfall of the Templars. The Franciscan rule of simplicity and austerity was similar to the rule adopted by the Knights themselves.

Leave the room by the far door and enter the Grand Gallery, which is where *The Da Vinci Code* intrigue begins.

Stand at the beginning of the gallery to admire the fabulous perspective of this great hall. It is here, about halfway along that "renowned curator Jacques Saunière" is murdered. He tore a Caravaggio from the wall to set off the museum alarm system, then stripped naked to splay himself like Leonardo's famous *Vitruvian Man*. He then drew a pentagram on his stomach with his own blood, a clue to the Sacred Feminine connection. To complete the picture he drew a circle around the circumference of his splayed limbs with a curator's black-light pen. He then wrote the scrambled Fibonacci sequence, followed by "O Draconian devil! Oh lame saint." Inspector Fache had rubbed out the "P. S. Find Robert Langdon." so when Langdon sees the crime scene, he is not aware that he is the prime suspect of the murder.

Sophie and Langdon decipher the code. The fact that the numbers are out of sequence is a clue that the letters have also been scrambled. *The Vitruvian Man*, recreated by Saunière's body, leads them to Da Vinci. Then the penny drops! The anagram makes "Leonardo Da Vinci, The Mona Lisa". Off Sophie goes to look at the *Mona Lisa*, where she discovers another anagram, "So Dark The Con of Man". This sends her on the trail of *The Madonna of the Rocks*. Behind this painting she finds the key marked P. S. (those letters again!) As Grouard, the security agent, prepares to shoot Langdon, Sophie begins to put her knee through the painting!

The tour continues, though not in the order of the events in the book as the paintings have been moved from their original locations, and may well be moved again at a later date.

Continue along the Grand Gallery, look out to the left for the Leonardo Da Vinci collection. The paintings are hung immediately after the first pair of white marble double columns. A short life of Leonardo follows the descriptions of his works.

You will see:

John the Baptist

Painted c. 1505-8. The figure seems quite androgynous, a type of beauty Leonardo had been interested in throughout his life. Some scholars have seen this as an example of ideas that assimilate John to Adam, before the division of the sexes, and as a reinterpretation of the myth of Hermaphrodite. Others see his smile as that of a fallen angel. His fleshy body, is unlike the usual image of an adult John, which is usually shown as emaciated after fasting in the desert. Here he is much more suggestive of a pagan god.

The Madonna of the Rocks

This painting was ordered by the brotherhood of the Immaculate Conception as the main altar piece for the newly built Church of San Francesco Grande in Milan. It was painted c. 1485. The picture was never delivered, and a second version was placed in the church, which is now in the National Gallery in London. It is possible that the church rejected the first version because the story that was illustrated was not clear enough. The holy figures have no halos, the angel has no wings and John the Baptist could

easily be confused with Jesus as he is being taken under the cloak of Mary and does not have his cross-shaped staff. The National Gallery version has all of these symbols, traditionally used to identify the various figures. Art historians have suggested that Leonardo was influenced by heretical ideas, especially those of Amadeo Mendes da Silva. He saw the Old Testament as prefiguring not Jesus, but John the Baptist and Mary, who was assimilated with "sophia" (➤ **See Isis chapter**).

The painting is especially admired for the beauty of the figures, with the delicacy of the "sfumato" shading technique, perfected by Leonardo, to give them the appearance of living breathing beings. This work was originally on wood but has been transferred to canvas. (This fact enabled Sophie to start pushing her knee through it to save Langdon from Grouard).

The Virgin and Saint Anne

This is an unfinished work which shows the flow of life between the Virgin, her mother St Anne, and the Christchild. This was sometimes shown as the Virgin and Child sitting on St Anne's knees. Here, the bodies of the two women are almost fused, and it seems as though the Virgin's arm is extended from her mother's shoulder. The Virgin tries to restrain the Child, who is slipping from her arms towards the lamb, the symbol of his sacrifice, from which she cannot protect him. The beautiful serene face of St Anne is reminiscent of the *Mona Lisa*, as is the mysterious rocky landscape behind the figures.

Portrait of a Woman known as *La Belle Ferronière*

Painted c. 1495. This elegant portrait takes its name from the jewel worn across the woman's brow, which was fashio-

nable in Lombardy at the time. Some scholars dispute that the work is by Leonardo and although the woman was once thought to be the mistress of Leonardo's patron Ludovico Sforza, this is now questioned. Her perfect oval face is characteristic of the Italian Renaissance ideal, but her enigmatic gaze, glancing to the right as she seems to turn towards the viewer, gives this work a special depth. The reflection of her red velvet dress in the warm glow of her cheek is particularly lovely.

Further along the gallery there is a superb portrait by Raphael of ***Baldassare Castiglione***. He wears a hat and has a long beard. The portrait is a homage to the *Mona Lisa*.

You will pass a painting by **Bronzino** *Christ apparaissant à Madeleine*. This shows Christ appearing to Mary Magdalene after the Resurrection. She is the first to see him and mistakes him for a gardener. Christ says, "Noli

me tangere" which means "Touch me not." He goes on to say, "But go to my brethren and say to them I ascend unto my father."

Carravagio; *The Fortune Teller* and *The Death of the Virgin*

There are several Caravaggios in the gallery and which one Saunière throws to the ground is not specified. In the light of his own devotion to Mary Magdalene it would be appropriate if it was *The Death of the Virgin*, but this huge canvas would be somewhat unwieldy!

Another beautiful painting by this artist is *The Fortune Teller*. It shows a wealthy young man having his palm read, while the gypsy fortune teller is stealing his ring.

The Death of the Virgin scandalised the Church because the artist had painted the scene with too much realism. He was accused of using a dead prostitute, fished out of the river Tiber, as a model! During this period, people were used to seeing the Virgin represented elegantly clothed, sitting on a cloud being transported up to heaven.

Caravaggio died at 37 having lived a tempestuous life. He killed a man in a brawl and died in a fit of rage. His paintings make bold use of chiaro-scuro, (the heightened contrast of light and dark), which adds drama to the scenes.

Continue along the Gallery towards the *Mona Lisa*.

Mona Lisa

Painted on a poplar wood panel c 1504. Sometimes called portrait of Mona Lisa Del Giocondo (hence the title *La Joconde* in French). Langdon mentions that her name is an anagram of Amon L'Isa, the divine union of male and female. This, he says, is the reason for her smile. It would seem that the work started as an actual portrait of the young wife of Del Giocondo. Leonardo's biographer Vasari writes of how singers and musicians were employed to entertain her while she modelled, to make her expression less melancholy. However, despite these details, it would seem that the portrait is of an ideal and not a specific person.

BIOGRAPHY OF LEONARDO DA VINCI (1452-1519)

Leonardo Da Vinci was the illegitimate son of a lawyer and a woman about whom little is known. He was born near the town of Vinci, and spent several years in the care of his grandmother, which has led people to speculate that he fused St Anne and the Virgin in the painting of this name because for him, grandmother and mother were one. When he was a child he had a dream that a bird of prey descended on him in his cradle. It opened his mouth with its tail feathers and moved them about between his lips. He took this as a sign that nature wanted to speak to men through his mouth. It was a dream he never forgot. Freud saw the shape of this bird of prey in the figure of the Virgin's robe in the painting of the Virgin and St Anne.

He was apprenticed to Verocchio in Florence at the beginning of his career as an artist. Verrocchio was fascinated by maths, alchemy and magic, and his studio was the centre of the most modern ideas of its day. Leonardo was remarkably beautiful, courteous, a bit effeminate and a loner. He had difficulty finishing his projects and paintings. Once he had solved an idea he wanted to move on. Leonardo was not highly educated, but he was interested in everything, and excelled in many disciplines. Like others in his time, he was intrigued by irrigation, hydraulics, war machinery, and he was also an accomplished musician. He wrote extensively on the theory of art, was fascinated by riddles and enigmas, and made extensive notes in a special script as he was left handed, called his "mirror writing". His contribution to art is to have produced the most beautiful figures representing feminine spirituality. He brought to perfection the "sfumato" style of gentle contours, where the figure is bathed in a soft light, which makes it look at one with its surroundings.

Leonardo worked for patrons such as Lorenzo the Magnificent in Florence, and Ludovico Sforza in Milan, and was eventually invited to France at the end of his life by the King, Francis I. He was given a mansion and a pension by the French king so that he could live comfortably, at the royal town of Amboise in the Loire Valley. Nothing was required of him except the pleasure of his conversation. Leonardo died and was buried in Amboise in 1519. The Mona Lisa seems to have been a favourite painting he did not wish to part with during his lifetime.

The pyramidal structure of the composition accentuates her brow, the seat of the intellect. The simplicity of her tunic, and her loose hair under a delicate veil, give the figure a timeless appeal, and leave room for the imagination. This is in contrast to the way portraits at the time generally show the status of the sitter by fashionable clothes and an elaborate interior. Her smile is extremely delicate, one of interior meditation.

In the background is a mysterious rocky landscape, with the imprint of man in the form of a road and a bridge (the winding path represents the journey of the soul). In the distance, the landscape is completely wild.

As Langdon points out, the horizon seems to be different on the left and the right of the figure. The reason for this is open to interpretation. The strokes of the paint brush are so delicate that they cannot be seen.

After visiting *Mona Lisa* walk back to the large format French paintings. Some of the museum's most famous 19th century works are located here including: Géricault's *Raft of the Medusa*, and *Delacroix's Liberty Leading the People*. Continue to Veronese's *Wedding at Cana*.

Wedding at Cana

Veronese's *Wedding at Cana* is the largest painting in the Louvre. In *Da Vinci Code* Theory, the wedding taking place is really between Christ and Mary Magdalene. In this version, Christ and Virgin Mary (the mother-in-law?!) sit in the centre of the painting, there is a bride and groom present, (can you pick them out from the crowd?).

The painting was commissioned by the Benedictines of San Giorgio in Venice as a decoration for their refectory, and it was delivered in 1563. One imagines the monks having their meagre meal with this sumptuous banquet taking place behind them. The painting immortalises the first of Christ's miracles when water is turned to wine. The 132 figures were painted in less than a year and the picture is rich in religious symbolism. The horizontal balustrade separates the terrestrial sphere from the heavens. Above Christ's head, between the posts of the balustrade, is a pilgrim's bottle, symbolic of the water that Christ turns to wine. Lamb is being carved above Christ's head, which represents Christ as the sacrificial lamb, even at the time of his first miracle. Beneath Christ is an hourglass, showing that time is running out and that the end of Christ's life approaches. The hourglass looks like an image of the Holy

Grail. Beneath this, two dogs chew at a bone, the symbol of death. The two dogs are chained together but one wishes to pull away but can't: this symbolises marriage!

High up on the right hand side, a hand throws carnations down to earth from heaven. The name for this flower refers to the Incarnation (Christ becoming flesh) and its red colour symbolises the Crucifixion. There are many dogs in the painting, including one up in the heavens that looks

straight at Christ. Dogs are often used to symbolise loyalty and fidelity which suits a marriage scene. Here, they are also believed to represent the creature to whom we throw terrestrial nourishment, which is in contrast to the spiritual nourishment offered by Christ.

Veronese's self portrait is said to be that of the viola player, and the master of ceremonies pouring the wine, is his brother Benedetto.

Other painters are thought to be portrayed here: Titian plays the contrabass, Tintoretto the violin and Bassano the flute.

Walk back the way you came, to the end of the "Large Format Gallery", go down the stairs marked "escalier Molien", at very bottom of the steps take a sharp right turn, go down again, following "entresol", "12th to 16th century Italian sculptures". Turn right into the northern sculpture.

St Mary Magdalene

At the entrance to room C is a beautiful carved and painted wooden statue of Mary Magdalene by the German artist Erhart. Here she is shown naked with long flowing hair. This symbolises Mary at the end of her life when she was living the life of a repentant hermit. The back of the sculpture contains a door to a small compartment.

At the far end wall there are two carved wooden altar pieces, the smaller one on the right hand side illustrates episodes from the life of Mary Magdalene in lively sculptures, and the larger one shows a scene of the Crucifixion. Mary Magdalene is at the foot of the cross with her alabaster jar of ointment.

Return to room 3, turn right and walk through Italian and Spanish sculptures. Opposite the exit as you leave, there is a beautiful primitive Italian tetramorph. Go down the steps, cross the hall and go up the steps into pre-classical Greece.

Room 1 pre-classical Greece

Here you see some very ancient idols, including the *Bell Shaped Idol*.

Continue through the gallery to room 3, turn right into room B, and follow the sign down the steps into room C. Here you will find yourself inside the reconstruction of a Coptic church.

This room was once the amphitheatre of the Louvre school, and has been reserved to house the generous gift from Egypt, the fragments of the Monastery church of Baouit. A scale model of the monastery stands in the middle of the room.

This site was excavated from middle Egypt by French archaeologists and dates from the 4th to the 12th centuries.

The Coptic Church is the Christian Church in Egypt. It is based upon the teachings of St Mark who brought Christianity to Egypt in the 1st century AD.

The Nag Hammadi texts, found in upper Egypt in 1945, are bound manuscripts, and are written in the Coptic language, which is still used by Coptic Christians in Egypt. These are the books known as the Gnostic Gospels.

The Dead Sea Scrolls are written in Hebrew and Aramaic, and were the records of an ascetic sect known as the Essenes. This sect lived at around the time of Jesus and John the Baptist. The Nag Hammadi texts, or Codices, were written slightly later, and were copied into Coptic from the Greek originals. The Coptic Church uses the looped cross called the Crux Ansata. This comes from the pagan Egyptian ankh. Paganism was still a strong force in the early Christian period. Back in room B, a small display cabinet labelled "Magie" shows hand written spells and incantations, and some lucky charms and figurines that have been stuck with pins like voodoo dolls.

Walk back through pre-classical Greece and return to the Pyramid. Your tour can finish here. Leave the Pyramid following the metro signs if you wish to see the inverted pyramid.

If you want to go into the Richelieu Wing, you can see the two following paintings that are an important feature of the book: *The Holy Blood and The Holy Grail.*

Nicolas Poussin

Top floor Richelieu Wing, 14th-17th century French paintings, room n° 14.

Et in Arcadia Ego c. 1640. *(The Arcadian Shepherds)*

This is one of Poussin's best known works. A group of shepherds and a classically dressed woman in the idyllic land of Arcadia come across a tomb on which they decipher the inscription Et in Arcadia Ego which means that even in Arcadia I (death) exist. One of the shepherds kneels down beside the tomb and traces the inscription with his finger.

This reminds them that death is present even in what seems to be paradise. The man and the woman on the right are discussing the idea, while the man on the left is absorbed in meditation.

This is an allegorical painting which has the same message as a "vanity" painting, which emphasises the ephemeral quality of human life, like the shadow of the shepherd who reads the inscription. There is no moral. The painting has a mood of elegiac poetry and was intended to provoke

a meditation on human frailty. Paintings on this theme often depict Mary Magdalene meditating with a skull or an oil lamp, the symbol of repentance. There is a beautiful painting by George de la Tour on this theme in the Louvre.

The mysterious manuscripts found by Saunière at Rennes-le-Château make coded references to both *Shepherds* and Poussin. The authors of *The Holy Blood and The Holy Grail* claim to have found the tomb and the landscape which figure in Poussin's painting, *The Arcadian Shepherds*. It is at Arques, near Rennes-le-Château!

Poussin's *Self Portrait,* (1650) (same room as above)

This sensitive work shows Poussin in a philosopher's gown, with slightly unkempt hair and a troubled look, surrounded by paintings, mostly hidden from view, and holding a portfolio of his drawings.

The work can be compared to other artists' self portraits where they are glorified and surrounded by the attributes of the arts to stress their many intellectual achievements.

Here Poussin shows only one detail of his work, which is emphasised for symbolic reasons: a woman in profile with a headdress decorated with one eye. She represents the art of painting, and the two outstretched arms which embrace her may represent Poussin embracing his profession, or his friendship for the man who commissioned the work. Poussin is wearing a ring with a diamond cut into a four sided pyramid, a common stoic symbol of constancy. Poussin was not interested in portraiture and was going to have the work done by another painter, but finally decided to paint it himself, thinking no one else would produce a painting to his satisfaction.

Château Villette and Beyond

The Last Supper

Château Villette

Château Villette is the magnificent property near Paris, where Leigh Teabing resides. He lives the expat's dream life having built himself a little England within the bounds of his French château. The actual château that inspired Brown is called the château de Villette, and is located near Pontoise in the heart of "Impressionist" countryside. It was built by the prestigious architect François Mansart, for the Count of Aufflay, who was Louis XIV's ambassador to Italy. Mansart had built some beautiful mansions and town houses in Paris, including his own which can be seen at 5 rue Payenne in the Marais. This extraordinary building has become the headquarters of the curious cult of Positivists. This is the only positivist meeting house in France, and is the location of their Chapel of Humanity. No Supreme Being is worshiped here, it is great men of the past that are meditated upon: Dante, Shakespeare, Descartes, Homer, Aristotle and Caesar. Their motto "Love as a principal, order as a basis, progress as a goal" is written on the front of the building. Mansart built his home here in 1622. He is also remembered for building the magnificent dome of the Oratory of the Val-de-Grace in Paris.

The château de Villette was finished in 1696 by Jules Hardouin-Mansart, the architect's grandnephew, who

also built the Hall of Mirrors at Versailles for the Sun King. The gardens of the Château de Villette are typical of the formal French style of Le Nôtre, with lovely lakes. They are appropriately home to an obelisk and a pair of sphinxes.

Famous People at the Château de Villette

In the 18th century, the château was owned by the Marquis de Grouchy. His daughter was married in the chapel here, and her name was Marie Louise Sophie! Her husband was Condorcet, a political theorist whose ideas were remarkably modern. He was a moderate at the Revolution and supported the idea of giving women the right to vote. His close friend La Fayette was a witness at the wedding. The story told at the Château is that M. L. Sophie and La Fayette fell in love at first sight, but La Fayette unable to be disloyal to his friend, left France with a broken heart for America! Apparently the lovely Sophie wasted no time in replacing him. Condorcet and La Fayette were both masons and held frequent masonic meetings here. During the Revolution, Condorcet, promoter of free education for all, and contributor to the great French *Encyclopaedia*, took his own life rather than be sent to the guillotine.

Famous Faces from Modern Times

The château is no stranger to the silver screen. Many films have been made here including *The Count of Monte-Cristo* starring Gérard Depardieu, and *Le Libertin* with Fanny Ardant.

It is highly likely that a recent American best-seller will be made here soon!

Today the château is privately owned, and has been beautifully restored and furnished. It is available for visits, weddings, and conferences. The present owner, Olivia Hsu Decker organises special Da Vinci Code holidays. These include staying in the luxurious accommodation offered at the château and some gourmet food.

➤ **For more information and booking:**
Local contact – Andrew Ryan 06 64 81 12 48
or andrew.ryan@laposte.net
e-mail: villette@frenchvacation.com
Tel: + 001 (415) 435.1600
Fax: + 001 (415) 383.1258

Other Local Curiosities

The Mummified Leg of Marie de Medici!

The musée Tavet in Pontoise exhibits an eclectic collection of curios. Both local history and modern art fill its galleries, but deep in the heart of its store-rooms is the mummified leg of the queen. The relic was saved during the revolutionary destruction of the royal tombs at Saint-Denis. It was later purchased by Mr. Tavet, who was a historian and scholar. He founded the museum and is its principal legator! When he died in 1892, his personal collection was donated to the museum. This included the leg of the queen. This fragile relic is not on general view.

➤ **The musée Tavet-Delacour, 4, rue Lemercier, 95000 Pontoise. Open Wednesday to Sunday 10am-12.30pm & 1.30pm-6pm.**

Écouen

Not far from Paris is the beautiful Renaissance château d'Écouen. The home was built for the head of the king's army, Duke Anne de Montmorency.

The collections here are fascinating and include the famous set of 16th century tapestries telling the story of David and Bathsheba. *The Dying Slaves* by Michelangelo once adorned the façade of the inner courtyard. There are many beautiful frescoes here, and a superb collection of Renaissance objects and furniture.

The most extraordinary exhibit is an exact replica of Leonardo Da Vinci's ***The Last Supper***, which is in the family chapel. This painting is of inestimable interest because although a copy, it is a contemporary work and probably the best representation anywhere of what Da Vinci's painting originally looked like.

The Da Vinci Code: Teabing Interprets *The Last Supper*

Having explained to Sophie that the Holy Grail is actually Mary Magdalene, he uses the following arguments from the painting to support the theory: each of the disciples has an individual wine glass, the chalice or cup, as described in the Bible, is not being passed among the grouped figures. The figure to the right of Christ is analysed as being a woman, "flowing red hair, delicate hands and the hint of a bosom. It was without a doubt... female." "That my dear." Teabing replied, "is Mary Magdalene." The two central figures wear inversed clothing and represent Yin and Yang. (The concept of masculine and femine being both essential parts of a whole.) The space between them forms a V shape, this is the chalice or Sacred Feminine symbol. The two figures, if seen as a whole, form a large letter M, which is the M for Mary Magdalene, the Grail that is present after all. Teabing argues that Christ in fact entrusted his Church to Mary Magdalene. Because of this, Peter, who was jealous, makes a cutting gesture at her throat. Teabing also describes a mysterious disembodied hand holding a knife.

Écouen is accessible by train from Paris-gare du Nord.

Journey time to Écouen-Ezainville station is about 25 minutes. The walk from the station to the château is a leisurely half hour. The museum is closed on Tuesdays.

Le Bourget

Teabing keeps his private jet here, and makes a quick getaway with stifled Silas bound and gagged in the back of the plane. It is here that they make their first attempts to open the cryptex.

Le Bourget was once a place of magic where the pioneering "magnificent men in their flying machines" would experiment. In the 30s, rich and fashionable jet-setters would fly into Paris via Le Bourget airfield. The Golden Age of romance is long gone, Le Bourget is today swallowed up in Paris' ever growing suburbs and is home to the Museum of Flight and Space Travel. Its horizon is dominated by the French rocket Arianne. The Anglo-French Concorde is part of the museum, and can be visited here.

The Spirit of St Louis

On the 21st of May 1921, Lindberg landed at Le Bourget at 10.22pm. After 33 and a half hours of flight he completed the first ever Atlantic crossing. This exploit had created enormous excitement in Paris, and it is reported that some 100,000 people were there waiting for him when he arrived. The French rewarded his incredible achievement by giving him the prestigious Legion of Honour. (➤ **See also American Embassy, see index**).

If you wish to visit Paris in the **Spirit of Langdon and Sophie**: contact Paris Helicoptere for a ride, departure from Le Bourget every Sunday, 25 minute tour of Paris 01 48 35 90 44, or try Montgolfière aventures for a more sedate visit but a bumpier landing. 01 40 47 61 04.

Chartres
The Town and the Cathedral

Chartres is located about 55 miles south west of Paris. It is easily accessible by train from Montparnasse Station, and the journey takes about an hour. Langdon has come to Paris to lecture on the pagan symbolism of the cathedral.

It was originally a pagan holy shrine and like many other churches is built on an ancient holy well. There is much to see here and it is worth planning to spend a whole day. Both the cathedral and the medieval town are beautiful. The town is bustling and there are plenty of restaurants and cafés for lunch. The local speciality is the Mentchikoff, a truffly chocolate coated in meringue. These are sold in attractive boxes illustrated with a picture of the cathedral. On arrival at Chartres, go straight to the Tourist Office and ask for a free map, which includes a guided tour of the old town. Headphone commentary can be hired to accompany the visit. Guided tours of the cathedral are given in English by local specialist Malcolm Miller. Ask for the tour programme at the Tourist Office.

A Guided Tour For Pagans and Christians

At Chartres, legend, myth and history mix to make the story that has come down to us today. The holy site has pagan origins and the first church here was built above the

Chartres Cathedral

pagan well. It is said that pre-Christian Druids practiced a virgin cult here.

There is evidence of a church being destroyed and rebuilt here as early as 743. Towards the end of the 8th century, Pepin the Bref, Dan Brown's insecure Merovingian shorty!, made a gift to the church of "Mary at Chartres". The city and church were sacked in the 9th century. A new church was built and consecrated in 876, and it was at this time that Chartres acquired its precious Holy Relic, the "Sancta Camisia". This veil, which is on display inside the church, is purported to have been worn by the Virgin Mary when she gave birth to Christ. At a time when the cult of the Virgin was gaining importance in Europe, this relic was a valuable asset capable of generating income for the church. It was also valuable protection for the city. When the Viking Rollon came to besiege the city, the veil was displayed before him, he and his men fled, then made peace and converted to Christianity. These men would become the great cathedral builders of Normandy, who gave their name to the Norman style of architecture.

Through the 10th and 11th centuries, Chartres became an extremely important and active centre of learning, and it remained so until the Sorbonne was founded in Paris. In the early 12th century, neo-Platonist Bernard of Chartres was one of the famous scholars. He saw the scholars of his time as dwarves perched on the shoulders of giants. The giants were the philosophers of the Ancient World. This theme is reflected in the decorative scheme of the façade.

Medieval education was divided into the seven liberal arts. These were divided into two sub-groups respectively the Trivium (3 branch) and the Quadrivium (4 branch). The mind was seen as being enlightened by the Quadrivium (mathematics, geometry, astronomy and music) and as expressing itself through the Trivium (grammar, rhetoric and dialectic). These are all represented on the royal portal of the cathedral.

The royal portal (1145-1155)

These are the oldest statues and carvings at Chartres. The royal portal is divided into three bays.

Central Portal

The tympanum shows Christ the Teacher in a mandorla surrounded by the tetramorph (➤ **See glossary**). The tetramorph represents the Evangelists who spread the teaching of Christ. The gesture Christ is making with his right hand signifies that he is speaking, and the book in his other hand shows that he is speaking about the Bible, ie. teaching.

Right Portal

The tympanum shows Christ as a child with the Virgin Mary. Beneath this, on the lintel, is the Presentation at the Temple, and beneath this, the Nativity. A shepherd in medieval stockings plays the pan-pipes while standing over his flock of archaic sheep.

Two ribbed archivolts surround the tympanum. The figures here represent the trivium and quadrivium. At the base of the inner archivolt, on the right-hand side, sits Pythagorus, and on the outer, Donatus. Above Pythagorus, Music plays bells, and above Donatus, Grammar beats her

lessons into boys with a birch stick. On the outer archivolt, on the left hand side, at the bottom, is Aristotle.

On the sculpted capitals wrapped around the buttress between the central and righthand portal is a lovely carved Last Supper, and just right of this is the Kiss of Judas.

Left-Hand Portal

The tympanum shows Christ's ascension. Beneath this can be seen beautiful flying angels. In the archivolt, one can see the labours of the month and the signs of the zodiac: starting bottom left outer, harvesting in July, above the harvest is the sign of Cancer. Bottom right inner, smelling flowers in spring, and above this is the symbol of Aries the ram. The complete zodiac can be followed all the way around the portal.

South Portal, left-hand bay. A carving of medieval knights beheading Thomas a Becket.

Holy Well

This is in the crypt and is 33 metres deep, it was undoubtedly the original Gallo-Roman well.

Isis and the Cult of Black Virgins

There were two black Virgins at Chartres, only one has survived. "Our Lady of the Crypt", was destroyed at the Revolution, but "Our Lady of the Pillar" is in the chapel at the angle of the choir and the north transept. The statue is made from painted pear wood and is probably from the 16th century. There are many of these statues in the south of France, and their origin is unknown. It is argued, however, that the black Virgin statues descend from the cult of Isis. The Virgin's crown of stars and association with water are both borrowed from the iconography of Isis.

L'Ane qui vielle Outside the Cathedral on the South Side

There is a sculpture of a donkey playing a hurdy gurdey. It is in poor condition and its symbolism remains obscure.

An Ancient Labyrinth

Just inside the cathedral is the beautiful and mysterious labyrinth. There were labyrinths like this in many cathedrals including Sens, Amiens, Arras and Reims. These were later removed because considered pagan. The labyrinth is defined by being the longest possible route in the shortest possible space. The line is several hundred metres long and pilgrims arriving here on the route to Compostella, would crawl along the line saying prayers on their hands and knees. It takes about an hour to complete this journey. It is also referred to as "The road to Jerusalem", but for the pagans, it was the journey of life ending in death. For the Christians, at least paradise was waiting at the end.

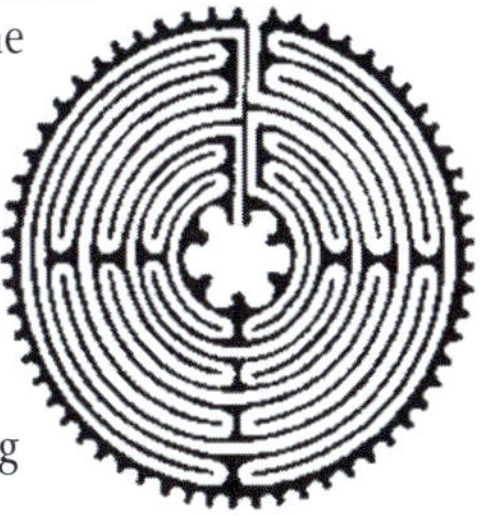

Corporations and Secret Signatures: The Windows

Each window at Chartres was given by a wealthy local corporation and includes the guild signature in the lower corners of the windows. These are fairly easy to identify. The Mary Magdalene Window (2nd window in the south side aisle) was given by the water carriers, and they can be seen in the bottom left and right-hand corners of the window. The water carriers have an affinity with Mary because she washed Christ's feet with her tears. The Good Samaritan Window (3rd in south aisle) was given by the shoemakers. They can be seen in their workshops in the bottom three panels of the window. The shoemakers of Chartres were very wealthy, as the pilgrims arriving on foot had to buy new footwear. Walk round the church to the north side aisle, starting at the first window, nearest the façade:

coopers, carpenters and wheelwrights, 2nd wine merchants, 3rd drapers and furriers, 4th bankers, 5th haberdashers and apothecaries, 6th blacksmiths.

The Famous Blue Virgin of Chartres can be seen in the first bay of the south side, after the transept crossing. This window is a relic of the ancient church which was found in the debris after the fire of 1194. Having survived the fire, the window was considered miraculous. It was paraded as a religious relic, along with the Sancta Camisia, to raise money for the rebuilding of the church. The 12th century panels were set in a new window. Two different colours of blue are apparent, the lighter 12th century blue is the famous "blue of Chartres". ➤ **See illustration p. 16.** The Sancta Camisisa is visible in a side chapel.

The Astrological Window Next to the Blue Virgin

This window was donated by both the vine-growers and Count Thibault of Champagne. Signs of the zodiac are shown in the medallions on the right, and the corresponding labours of the month are on the left. The central medallions show both a sign and the seasonal labour. January is shown with three heads, looking at the past, present and into the future.

The west façade windows, beneath the main rose, are from left to right: the tree of Jesse, the Incarnation, the Passion and the Resurrection.

The west rose tells the story of the Last Judgement.

➤ **Rooftop visit: you can climb to the roof for superb views across the city's rooftops and the magnificent plains of the Beauce region.**

Rennes-le-Château

At the heart of the mystery on which *The Da Vinci Code* is based is the ancient hill-top town of Rennes-le-Château. The story of the abbé Saunière and his mysterious finds is told in detail in *The Holy Blood and The Holy Grail* by Baigent, Leigh and Lincoln. This book should be on the reading list of anyone interested in the issues raised in *The Da Vinci Code*. The town is located in the Aude region of France, famous for its associations with the Cathars and Templars. At Rennes-le-Château, the principal sites open to the public are: the village, the church of Mary Magdalene with its strange carvings and inscriptions, and Saunière's house. Waxwork figures made by Grévin and several other curios can be seen, including: a neolithic carved sacrificial altar and a carved stone slab known as the Knights' Stone. The Wisigothic pillar in which Saunière found the hidden documents, is on display, as is a special hollow lectern with a secret cavity. The Magdala Tower and Saunière's private chapel are also open. Check with the Tourist Office before planning a trip. Opening hours vary and are reduced during off peak seasons.

The Cathedral of Notre Dame

Index

Metro

The metro is the cheapest and easiest way to travel. A "carnet" of ten tickets is good value, (pronounced car-nay). Weekly travel passes can be purchased, but only run Monday to Sunday. The day pass "Paris Visite" is only worth while if you are making more than the ten "carnet" journeys. The carnet has no date limit and can be used on the bus, the metro, and the Montmartre funicular lift. Journeys on the RER can have different tariffs if leaving zone 1, 2 or 3. Supplements are necessary for Versailles and the airports.

Museum Pass

The museum pass is good value if you wish to visit two or more museums in a day, and it is valid for 1, 3 or 5 days. The pass is available at major metro stations and most museums. It gives priority entrance to permanent collections, but does not include temporary exhibits. It may be purchased in advance and is validated as of your first museum visit.

Museums

Most museums in Paris are closed either Mondays or Tuesdays. Some are free the first Sunday of the month. Many museums are free for under 18s (bring ID).

ART AND HISTORY

Arc de Triomphe, 75008, metro Charles-de-Gaulle-Étoile, open every day.

Arch of la Défense, metro Grande-Arche, open every day.

Archaeological Crypt Notre-Dame, place du Parvis, 75004, metro Cité, closed Mondays.

Bibliothèque nationale de France-F.-Mitterrand, 11, quai François-Mauriac, 75013, metro Bibliothèque François-Mitterrand, closed Mondays.

Bibliotheque nationale de France-Richelieu, 58, rue de Richelieu, 75002, metro Bourse, closed Mondays.

Catacombs, 75014, metro Denfert-Rochereau, closed Mondays.

Chapelle expiatoire, 29, rue Pasquier, 75008, metro Havre-Caumartin, Thursdays, Fridays and Saturday afternoons.

Cluny Medieval Museum, 6, pl. Paul-Painlevé, 75005, metro Cluny-la-Sorbonne, closed Tuesdays.

Cognac-Jay Museum (18th century), 8, rue Elzevir, 75003, metro St Paul, closed Mondays.

Conciergerie (museum of the Revolution), 4, bd du Palais, 75001, metro Cité, open every day.

Dali Museum, 11, rue Poulbot, 75018, metro Abbesses, open every day.

Delacroix Museum, 6, rue de Furstemberg, 75006, metro St Germain-des-Prés, closed Tuesdays.

Eiffel Tower, 75007, metro Champs-de-Mars, open every day 9.30am-11pm.

Eroticism (Museum of), 72, bd de Clichy, 75018, metro Blanche, open every day.

Fakes Museum (Contrefaçon), 16, rue de la Faisanderie, 75016, metro Porte-Dauphine, closed Monday.

Fashion Museum (palais Galliera), 10, av. Pierre-Ier-de-Serbie, 75016, metro Iéna, closed Tuesdays, open for special exhibitions only.

Freemasonry Museum, 16, rue Cadet, 75009, closed Sundays and Mondays.

Glasses and Lorgnettes Museum, 85, rue du Faubourg-St-Honoré, 75008, metro Concorde, Open Tuesday-Saturday 10am-12pm & 2pm-6pm.

Invalides (Military Museum), 75007, metro Invalides, closed 1st Monday of every month.

Jacquemart-André (18th century and Renaissance + restaurant), 158, bd Haussmann, 75008, metro Miromesnil, open every day.

Jeu-de-Paume, (Contemporary Art), 75001, metro Concorde, closed Mondays. Temporary exhibitions only.

Le Corbusier (Villa La Roche), 8, square du Docteur-Blanche, 75016, metro Jasmin, closed Sundays and Monday am.

Letters and Manuscripts Museum, 8, rue de Nesle, 75006, metro Odéon, closed Mondays and Tuesdays.

Louvre Museum, 75001, metro Palais-Royal-Musée-du-Louvre, closed Tuesdays.

Maillol Museum, 61, rue de Grenelle, 75007, metro rue-du-Bac, closed Tuesdays.

Marmottan Museum, (Impressionists especially Monet), 2, rue Louis-Boilly, 75018, metro La Muette, closed Mondays.

Money and the Mint, (La Monnaie) 11, quai Conti, 75006, metro Pont-Neuf, closed Mondays.

Montmartre Museum, 12, rue Cortot, 75018, metro Lamarck, closed Mondays.

Notre Dame, Cathedral Towers, metro Cité, open every day.

Orsay Museum, metro Solferino, closed Mondays.

Pantheon (Foucault's Pendulum), place du Panthéon, 75005, metro Maubert-Mutualité, open every day.

Playing Card Museum, 16, rue Auguste-Gervais, 92130 Issy-les-Moulineaux, metro Mairie-d'Issy, closed Mondays and Tuesdays and Friday am (Tarots).

Police Museum, 4, rue de la Montagne-St-Genevieve, 75005, metro Maubert-Mutualité, closed Sundays.

Pompidou Centre, 75004, metro Chatelet-les-Halles, closed Tuesdays.

Sainte-Chapelle, 4, bd du Palais, 75001, metro Cité, open every day.

Radio France Museum, 116, av. du President-Kennedy, 75016, metro Ranelagh, closed Saturdays and Sundays, must reserve 01 56 40 15 16.

The Tower of John the Fearless, 20, rue Étienne-Marcel, 75002, metro Étienne-Marcel, Wednesday, Saturday and Sunday afternoons.

Sewers Museum (les Egouts), left bank end of Alma bridge, 75007, metro Alma-Marceau, closed Thursdays and Fridays, and the last three weeks of January.

Paris Story, multimedia show, 11 bis, rue Scribe, 75009, metro Opéra, open every day, show every hour.

Victor Hugo Museum, 6, place des Vosges, 75004, metro St Paul, closed Mondays, entrance free.

RELIGION

Mosque of Paris, place du Puits-de-l'Hermite, 75005, metro Jussieu, closed Tuesdays.

Guimet Museum (Asiatic Art and Buddhism), 6, place d'Iéna, 75016, metro Iéna, closed Tuesdays.

Jewish Art and History Museum, 71, rue du Temple, 75003, metro Rambuteau, closed Saturdays.

Notre Dame Museum, 10, rue du Cloître-Notre-Dame, 75004, metro Cité, Wednesdays, Saturdays and Sundays.

Arab World Institute (Pre and post-Islamic culture), 1, rue des Fossés-St-Bernard, 75005, metro Jussieu.

Food

Good food is available everywhere in Paris. Avoid the most touristy areas for anything other than a snack. The Champs-Élysées and Concorde areas tend to be especially expensive for food, coffees and light meals. Look at the food already on people's plates to see if it looks like something that you may enjoy. If a restaurant is filled with locals and does not display an English menu outside it is a good sign. A restaurant should always display a menu with prices outside the establishment. Ask for "la carte", the English word a "menu" means a fixed priced menu with limited choice of starters, main course and dessert. The "plat du jour", or dish of the day, is usually fresh. The Latin Quarter, Montmartre and the Marais have some of the best and most reasonable restaurants. A few restaurants are mentioned in this guide, however, they are included because of the appropriate and fun nature of their theme or décor rather than the food. Good restaurant guides are available from the English bookshops recommended in this guide. The quality of restaurants changes quickly, so purchase an up-to-date guide if you are keen on good food.

Tipping and Café Etiquette

An astonishing number of guide books say not to tip in cafés and restaurants as service is included. Watch the locals and you'll see how wrong this is! Clients leave a few small coins in the change saucer after a quick coffee, a couple of euros after a lunch, and more after a restaurant meal. If you order at the bar, stay at the bar, if you wish to sit down, order from the table. Drinks are cheaper at the bar, this is why you should not take them to a table. Service is included, usually at 15 percent, but this is not a tip, it is the waiters wage. Most waiters in cafés and brasseries get paid a small retaining wage, plus 15 percent of their daily takings. This charge is not included if you buy at the bar because the barman is effectively giving his service for free. If you have had nice service, leave a small gesture. Taxi drivers should also get to keep some change!

Taking a Cab

Cab drivers around the world have their own reputations. When travelling in a strange city it is easy to get the impression that a driver has taken you on a lengthy wild goose chase. Most drivers have better things to do and no shortage of clients! If you are worried about this then ask for a "fiche" as you get in, this is a receipt which records the starting and dropping point, price and driver's reference. If you find that you can't flag a cab down, then you are probably within a couple of minutes walk from a cab station.

Taking a Train

Train tickets can be bought at all railway stations, either at the "guichet" counter or by credit card from automatic distributors.

There is an SNCF (French Rail) counter in the Tourist Office by the inverted pyramid in the Louvre, and there are usually very few people in line there, and tickets are available for all over France and for Eurostar.

The English Language Bookstores

The Red Wheelbarrow, 22, rue St Paul, metro St Paul. Village Voice, 6, rue Princesse, metro Mabillon (around the corner from St Sulpice), San Francisco Bookstore, 17, rue Monsieur-le-Prince, metro Mabillon or Odéon. Tea and Tattered Pages, 24, rue Mayet, metro Duroc.